Cold Hearted Bitch : The True Story of Lynn Turner

Kelly Cobb

Published by Trellis Publishing, 2021.

While every precaution has been taken in the preparation of this book, the publisher assumes no responsibility for errors or omissions, or for damages resulting from the use of the information contained herein.

COLD HEARTED BITCH : THE TRUE STORY OF LYNN TURNER

First edition. July 16, 2021.

ISBN: 979-8224873548

Written by Kelly Cobb.

COLD HEARTED BITCH : THE TRUE STORY OF LYNN TURNER

KELLY COBB

The only thing that Lynn Turner loved more than a man in uniform was the act of killing one.

A certified cop killer, she would go on to marry and murder two different police officers in two different counties.

It started in 1995 when her husband Glenn Turner came into an emergency room claiming he was "sick with the flu." He would die one day later.

The same affliction would befall her common-law-husband, Randy Thompson.

Despite the parallels between the two cases, police still had difficulty proving the case. Lynn Thompson had failed to become a police officer years earlier and made a vow to "outsmart" the people who rejected her by committing the perfect murder.

This is how she tried to do it.

Julia Lynn was given up for adoption at birth and taken in by the Womack family on July 13th, 1968. Her adopted mother, Helen, was a legal secretary and the couple spoiled Lynn as much as they could. They bought her the most expensive toys and clothes they could afford. Unfortunately, the Womacks divorced when she was five and Helen would take full custody of Lynn. Helen would remarry but Lynn did not get along with her new step-father, D.L. Gregory.

As Lynn reached her teen years, she got caught up in drugs. The addiction soon got out of control and she was sent to a drug rehabilitation clinic in Atlanta.

Lynn would eventually graduate high school and begin working as a police dispatcher in addition to having a civilian position working with an undercover narcotic unit in Chattanooga. Lynn loved the police and firefighter culture, hanging out with them outside of work.

"She used to drive around in a Camaro," forensic psychologist Paula Orange said. "She wore tight pants and blouses, showing off her curvaceous bust. She also spent a lot of money she didn't have. For her, it was all about the appearance of being someone better than what she really was."

She would go to bars, hot tubs and shoot pool with the various men in uniform. One night, she would meet Cobb County police officer Glenn Turner at a house party in suburban Atlanta.

"It started out as a one night stand," Orange said. "Unfortunately for Glenn, it didn't stay that way. He became obsessed with the sexy Lynn and fell into her web. Lynn was not the most attractive girl that Glenn had come across. There were women in his church that were better looking than she was. But she had a way of dialing into what a man wanted."

Lynn was smitten with Glenn and began pursuing him aggressively. She would buy him exotic snakeskin cowboy boots as a gift coupled with tickets to baseball and NASCAR. Glenn's friends were suspicious as Glenn was not exactly a ladies man. He had a spare tire and was nicknamed "Buddha" because of jowly appearance.

"I'm sure Glenn didn't think that he could get that type of woman," Roswell detective Sylvia Browning said. "He felt she wasn't in his league and that she was a great catch."

"Glenn grew up in a Christian culture," Orange said. "He was taught to respect and court women. Then along comes Lynn and he does not have to do any of that. She's doing all the work. She does all of the seducing and all of the courting. He was the one swept off his feet."

Glenn's group of police friends (who referred to themselves as the "Rat Pack"), noticed that Lynn was also a big spender.

They had her pegged as a gold-digger but if Glenn was happy they would go along with it.

"She flirted with everybody," Glenn's friend Donald Cawthon said. "She often seemed to need to be the center of attention."

She also had a temper to go along with her flirtatious nature.

"She had an ability to go from being sweet to being hateful within seconds," Glenn's sister, Linda Hardy said.

Both his sister and family alike thought that the couple had very little in common aside from being NASCAR fans. They would go to the races together and Glenn would buy Lynn a pace car similar to the one they used at the Dayton 500.

BIGGER DREAMS

Lynn was described as someone who wanted a champagne diet on a beer budget. She didn't like being a "mere dispatcher" and had bigger dreams of better status. She wanted to be looked at as a "somebody" rather than another working class stiff. Lynn told Glenn of her desire to become a police officer and quit her dispatcher job.

"She wanted entrance into that clique," Orange said. "To be fully accepted. I think Lynn always felt like an outsider as more and more female officers entered the ranks."

Lynn was physically fit and she easily passed the physical tests on the police officer exam. She would fail the psychological exam, however. This failure would prove devastating to her psyche.

She did not want to go back to work as a dispatcher, telling Glenn that she felt it was "humiliating" after she had tried to go out for a police officer and failed. She then began snooping around the city for a more prestigious job but nothing came up. Faced with no other options, Lynn began calling in sick frequently for her dispatch job.

While on the job, her flirting with other officers did not stop. His brothers in blue didn't follow up on Lynn's offer out of respect for Glenn who was well-liked on the force. Still, his fellow officers worried about him as he showed up to work one day to show off an expensive engagement ring he had purchased. The ring was more than he could afford on his cop's salary but he bought it anyway, determined to propose to Lynn on Christmas day.

"He pulled out that little ring box, and I said, 'Oh, you have lost your damn mind,'" Cawthon said.

Lynn would agree to the marriage and they would move in together with a wedding targeted for August of 1993. Before the marriage vows were consummated, however, Lynn convinced Glenn to name her as the beneficiary on his insurance policies. It took some prodding and cajoling but he finally relented.

Word got back to his friends about the arrangement and they were all shocked.

They believed Glenn should have known better as Lynn was already in a ton of debt. She had a mortgage and car payment that nearly exceeded her monthly pay as a dispatcher. She was also saddled with penalty charges on her over-the-limit spending on both her credit cards and checking account.

She was looking for a meal ticket and Glenn was all too eager to provide.

WEDDING DAY & HONEYMOON

Glenn's family and friends all looked ill at ease at the wedding.

"Lynn is a strange girl," Glenn's mother Kathy said.

During the ceremony, the couple was unable to light the unity candle. Glenn's brother James thought that it would be a portent of things to come.

"I feel like I'm more at a funeral than a wedding," James said during his awkward speech as best man. "I don't see this working out, but I hope for the best."

Glenn's friends began taking bets on how long their friend would last.

Lynn's gold-digger ways would manifest themselves immediately after the wedding vows were exchanged. She chastised Glenn for booking a family cruise instead of the "luxury one". Their sex life wasn't much better as Glenn confided to his friends that Lynn had "female problems" and that their once robust sex life had grounded to a halt.

Six months into their marriage, the two began sleeping in separate bedrooms.

"Despite being in law enforcement and having street smarts," Orange said "Glenn seemed blind to all of the warning signs going on around him. Rather than take a step back and say, 'there is something wrong here', he blamed himself for all of their problems. He thought by catering to her every whim that she would see the light and try to make things work. He didn't have the life experience with women to realize that tactic does not work."

"He'd call her while we were working and say, 'Hey, can I bring you something to eat?'" fellow officer David Dunkerton said. "Most of the time she was downright rude to him. He'd hang up and say, 'Why do I even bother?'"

LET THE SPENDING BEGIN

Lynn acted as if she didn't have a care in the world. She financed a Datsun 240Z and began booking exotic vacations. Glenn could not keep up. He took an extra job as a gas station attendant just to keep up with Lynn's spending.

He bought nothing for himself.

"Lynn put him on a budget the last year of his life," Glenn's sister Linda said. "Twenty bucks a week."

After a few months, Glenn became convinced that Lynn would never see the light. Glenn mentioned divorce and then Lynn threatened to "shoot him with his own gun."

Fearing for his own safety, Glenn again confided in longtime partner Dunkerton. He told his friend that if anything happened to him, to immediately look at Lynn.

Lynn would go back and forth between her home in Cobb County with Glenn and her original hometown of Cumming, Georgia. It was there she would begin an affair with Randy Thompson, a Forsyth County firefighter. Glenn did not know of Lynn's infidelity but was already making arrangements for a divorce.

But before he could file papers he would inexplicably fall ill. On March 2nd, 1995 he was transported to the emergency room complaining of the "flu."

The staff treated him over the course of a few hours and he left the facility feeling better.

But when Lynn came home the next day, she found him dead in his bed.

The coroner chalked Glenn's death to "natural causes due to an irregular heartbeat."

She would collect over $150,000 from her husband's life insurance and receive his pension from the police department.

MOVING ON UP

Glenn's mother, Kathy, was suspicious about her son's death. Glenn was a healthy young man with no health issues and only thirty-one years old. He could not have died from "natural causes."

She looked at the autopsy report and wanted to know what the green substance was in Glenn's stomach at the time of his death. She thought it could be the Jell-O that Lynn fed him and wanted a further examination.

She was then told that further testing could be done but only by an outside agency which would cost a few thousand dollars.

Kathy, who worked as a house cleaner, did not have that kind of money and her questions went unanswered.

Glenn's fellow Rat Pack friends had their suspicions as well, commenting on how Lynn didn't shed one tear at his funeral.

"I've got to get the hell out of here," Lynn said before walking out hand-in-hand with another police officer.

Four days later, unknown to Glenn's family and friends, Lynn moved in with her lover, Randy Thompson.

Randy did not know that Lynn was married. They met through a mutual friend and hit it off. She plied him with gifts, just as she did Glenn, and took him on a luxury cruise.

"I couldn't understand why she was chasing Randy the way she was," Randy's mother, Nita Thompson said. "At first, he wasn't interested. But she was very, very persistent. She told all of us, including Randy, that she was divorced."

Randy Thompson had one daughter and worked as a Forsyth County Sheriff deputy when he first met Lynn. He would later achieve his lifelong dream of becoming a firefighter.

He had a similar personality to Glenn in that he was a jolly and kind man who deferred to women.

"He fit her archetype," Orange said. "She had the ability to target men that she knew she could win over with gifts and attention. Men who were unused to a woman pursuing them. Then once they were in her web she would flip the script. They would become the ones catering to her."

After Lynn won over Randy, she began working on his family. During their first Christmas together she splurged and bought members of his family extravagant gifts.

"She bought us all kinds of stuff," Nita Thompson said. "A CD and stereo combined. Gifts for my daughters. We had just met her and she's buying us all this extravagant stuff."

Lynn knew how to manipulate. It all came naturally to her. From the moment she was born, she herself was showered with gifts and knew how it could often be a method to get people to lower their guard. Even Thompson's mother Nita would later concede that she thought Lynn was a good mother to the children she would bear with her son.

SECOND TIME IS A CHARM

Lynn treated Randy better than she treated Glenn...at least in the beginning of their relationship.

"She bought all of this new stuff," Nita Thompson said. "She bought him a new car. Bought all kinds of stuff and finally, I asked her 'How can you afford all this?' and she said it was from an inheritance from her grandmother."

But the truth was she was purchasing all of these items from collecting Glenn's life insurance. These purchases would include a large ranch style home in Cumming, Georgia.

"Lynn had to have the best in life," Orange said. "She needed the biggest home, the flashiest car. Next came the children. She was fashioning the life that she wanted. If someone got in the way of that, watch out."

In January of 1996 , Lynn would give birth to a daughter, Amber. A year later, she would bear Randy another child, a boy named Randy.

Randy wanted to marry Lynn but she refused. He went so far as to give her an engagement ring but she never wore it. Her refusal to wear the ring hurt him a lot.

Lynn didn't want to marry Randy as she would become ineligible for Glenn's pension. But, true to form, she convinced Randy to add her as the beneficiary of his life insurance policy. He reluctantly agreed to the request and then she prodded him to increase the policy amount from $100,000 to $200,000.

Randy consented to the increase but then saw Lynn's behavior worsen. The two would fight on a regular basis and on one occasion Randy punched her in the mouth. She charged him with battery and he was fined $400 with ten months probation.

"Lynn specialized in finding emotionally fragile men," Orange said. "She found one in Randy who suffered from alcoholism after his first marriage ended. She knew how to play him and reportedly did so on a regular basis, making his life miserable."

Randy would drink heavily and took an overdose of pills during his time with Lynn. His family and friends thought he did it to get Lynn's attention. Friends would comment that their relationship seemed to work together when Randy "needed" her. Lynn needed Randy to be reliant on her for his emotional needs. When she didn't get it, the couple would fight.

"Randy had his own issues," Orange said. "These issues dated back to his first marriage. When he married Lynn, he tried to commit suicide a few times. But these looked to be simply attention-getting gestures. She had abused him emotionally to the point where he felt it necessary to try and kill himself to get her to be nice to him. So she had the power in the relationship. He was this big, bear of a man. An intimidating looking former sheriff and firefighter. But this petite woman had more power over him."

In 1999, just like Glenn, Randy would have enough and leave Lynn.

"I'm leaving for my own sanity," Randy told a friend.

His conscience got to him quickly over a few weeks. He decided he wanted to reconcile just for the sake of the children. They were only five and two years old at the time.

"It was difficult for Randy to leave the kids," Orange said. "It just broke the man's heart. He had to leave the kids and then negotiate with the cold-hearted Lynn to see them again. She was breaking him down mentally."

"If he (Randy) did the slightest thing to make her mad," Nita Thompson said. "She wouldn't let him see them (the children)."

Randy also began experiencing health problems. He suffered from a staph infection and had a stent inserted near his heart. Still, he recovered and came out of his illness with a renewed hope that things could be reconciled.

Lynn agreed to Randy's request to have a family dinner at the Longhorn Steakhouse in town.

They would then go back to Lynn's house for dessert but Randy would not spend the night.

"I asked him how things went," Nita Thompson said. "And he said 'not well.'"

Days later, Randy began to experience several abdominal pain and vomiting. He went to the emergency room but was later discharged home.

In his apartment alone, he telephoned his firefighter friend, Paul Adams.

Adams arrived to find the entire apartment a veritable mess. There was overturned furniture and various items on the floor.

Randy was hysterical.

"Do you think I'm going to die?" Randy asked.

The following morning, another firefighter friend, Barry Head, would find Randy dead.

He had been complaining of flu symptoms and had visited the emergency room earlier in the day. Similar to Glenn, he had extreme abdominal pain and was vomiting. The hospital released him into Lynn's care.

"She had 'nursed' him in the same way she had 'nursed' Glenn," Orange said. "She gave him tea and soup. Then some Jell-O. She had poisoned all of his food, however."

Randy did not show up for work the day after having 'dessert' with Lynn. His co-workers became worried.

"Several of his friends called," Randy's mother, Nita Thompson said. "And several of his friends went over to see why he wasn't answering his phone calls."

Randy's firefighter friends arrived at his home, peering through the window blinds. They could see Randy on the couch appearing to be asleep. They knocked and knocked to no avail.

Worried, they kicked the door down, hoping to revive their friend.

But Randy had been dead for hours.

He was only thirty-two years old.

"He and I were very close," Nita Thompson said. "He was my first-born and my only son."

Lynn showed no emotion when told of Randy's death. Her friends chalked up it to her "stuffing" her emotions as she could often come across as a "cold fish."

"Lynn was a psychopath who could only display a limited amount of emotions," Orange said. "She could fake happiness. But she couldn't fake sorrow. She couldn't feel it and she didn't know how to fake it, unlike some other female killers."

A BLACK WIDOW BITES

The coroner would again write off Thompson's death as "natural causes due to an irregular heartbeat."

The day before his funeral, Lynn contacted Randy's insurance company. She tossed the phone at the wall in anger when she found out that Randy's policy had been canceled as he had not been paying the premiums.

She instead only collected $36,000.

Soon, however, she would have other things to worry about. The parallels between Randy's and Glenn's death were too similar not to be ignored. Someone had to notice something...

That someone was Mike Archer, Glenn's former sergeant. He got in touch with Glenn's mother and vowed justice. His mother told him that she knew the truth all along but didn't know how to proceed.

Armed with the new information about Randy's death, the Rat Pack began a phone campaign to alert authorities of their suspicions about Lynn.

News media got hold of the story and began referring to Lynn as the "messenger of death" and a "black widow."

Randy Thompson's mother would receive a sympathy letter from Glenn Turner's mother saying that her son died of the same thing. Neither mother knew that both of their sons were intimately involved with Lynn Turner. The two began to exchange notes about what their sons had gone through and immediately put two and two together.

Lynn Turner had killed their sons. Not the flu.

A blood test was done on Thompson which would reveal the ethylene glycol based anti-freeze in his system.

"She had poured anti-freeze into his Jell-O," Orange said. "The anti-freeze was both colorless and odorless. If anything, it had a sweet taste. It would blend right in with his Jell-O, tea or soup. All she needed was about a third of a cup to poison the men. It would crystallize in their liver and cause a very painful death."

Further investigation would reveal that Lynn visited a local animal shelter, asking off-hand about what type of poison they used to put animals down.

"They told her about the 'purple liquid' they used to put down strays," Orange said. "Lynn inquired further and was told that the same chemicals existed in anti-freeze."

The police knew they were onto to something after they found the anti-freeze in Thompson's system. They then exhumed Glenn's body and found the exact same substance in his kidneys.

Crime scene photos from Glenn Turner's death would have a picture taken in the garage where the anti-freeze was visible.

"No one put two and two together at the time," Orange said. "To them, it was just a container of anti-freeze on the shelf in the garage. A typical sight."

ARREST AND CONVICTION

Lynn would be arrested for Glenn's murder ten months after she killed Randy. She would sit and listen with a bored facial expression as the prosecution built their case against her. Outside the courtroom, however, she would joke and laugh with reporters, boasting that she would go free.

"Lynn learned how to fake certain emotions," Orange said. "She is one of those people that I think are born bad. She didn't do what she did solely because of the money with the life insurance or what not. There was something else at play, especially when she was refused entry into the police force. She wanted to prove how much smarter she was than them. She truly believed that."

"She would have gotten away with the first murder. But she did it twice. But for the Thompson murder, she would have gotten away with murdering Glenn. God knows what else she did in her life to warrant her arrogance. She was never caught for anything until the second murder."

Lynn would be tried for Glenn's murder in 2004 and be found guilty. She would again go to trial in 2007 for Randy's murder and be convicted.

Lynn would be sentenced to life in prison without parole, serving out her time at the Metro State Prison in Georgia.

On August 30th, 2010, Lynn was found "unresponsive" in her jail cell and could not be revived. Her death would be ruled a suicide. She had accumulated enough of her blood-pressure medication pills to ingest and she overdosed.

Lynn's mother, Helen, visited her the previous Sunday and had her own suspicions on what happened to her daughter. Helen said that she feared for her daughter's safety as she alluded to being threatened by other inmates.

"As I started to leave," Helen recalled. "She said, 'Momma, those girls are going to get me. I just know they will.'"

An autopsy would later reveal no signs of foul play.

Glenn's friends still gather each year at his grave.

JUDY BUENOANO

15

Judy Buenoano loved men. But she loved killing them more.

In 1971, she murdered her husband James and nine years later she would kill her own son, Michael. In 1983, she would attempt but fail to kill her boyfriend, John Gentry. She is also believed to have been responsible for the death of Bobby Joe Morris (another boyfriend) in 1978. She was never convicted of the Morris crime, however, as by the time the authorities had connected the dots she was sentenced to death for the murder of her first husband.

But the suspicions didn't stop with the Morris death. Buenoano is also suspected of killing a man in 1974 and in 1980, another boyfriend would die under suspicious circumstances.

Buenoano would become the first woman executed in Florida since 1848 and only the third woman executed since capital punishment had been reinstated in 1976.

She would be sent to the electric chair in 1998. Her last words were that she wanted to be remembered as a "good mother."

Instead, she would go down as one of the most sadistic female serial killers in American history.

This is her story.

EARLY LIFE

Judy was born Judias Welty in Quanah, Texas on April 4th, 1943. Her father was a day laborer at a local farm. Judy would talk about her mother being a full-blooded member of the Mesquite Apache tribe but little did she know that a "Mesquite Apache" tribe didn't exist.

Her mother would die of tuberculosis when Judy was only two years old. She and her baby brother Robert would be sent to live with their grandparents while their two older siblings would be put up for adoption.

"When Judy's mother died," forensic psychologist Paula Orange said. "It sent Judy's life into a tailspin. This is one of those 'Butterfly Effect' scenarios. A tragic circumstance that occurred early in a child's life that led to her perpetuating pain on everyone else for the rest of her own adult life."

She would eventually leave her grandparents and join her father in Roswell, New Mexico. He had remarried and Judy would claim that both he and her new stepmother would beat, starve, and burn her with cigarettes.

They made her a "house slave", forcing her to do chores around the house at their bidding. Judy would finally act out at the age of fourteen as she would burn two of her step brothers with hot grease. Not stopping there, she attacked both her father and step-mom with fists flying.

Police would be called and Judy would be jailed for over two months. After she served her jail time, the judge gave Judy a choice, either return home or go to reform school. She opted for the latter and was sent to Foothills High School. She would remain there until 1959 when she would graduate at the age of sixteen.

She held her entire family in contempt, particularly her younger brother Robert.

"I wouldn't spit down his throat if his guts were on fire," Judy once said when asked about her brother.

CHANGING IDENTITY

Judy returned to Roswell but changed her name to "Anna Schultz". She found work as a nurse aide and would give birth to a baby boy out of wedlock, Michael Schultz on March 30, 1961. Judy would remain silent on the identity of the baby's father but people believed that Judy was having an affair with a pilot from the nearby air force base.

In 1963, the twenty-two-year-old Judy would marry James Goodyear. Goodyear was twenty-nine years old and serving as a sergeant in the United States Air Force.

They would have their first child together, James Jr, four years later. James would celebrate the event by legally adopting Michael. Daughter

Kimberly would come a year later as the family would move to Orlando, Florida.

Judy would then open her own business, starting the Conway Acres Child Care Center in Orlando. She listed James as the co-owner even though he was during a one-year tour in the Vietnam War. After returning home, he only had three months of downtime before he was admitted to the U.S. Naval Hospital in Orlando, complaining from symptoms staff physicians never quite identified. He would die on September 15, 1971.

Goodyear was only thirty-seven years old at the time of death and authorities believed he died due to natural causes.

"He came home from Vietnam ill and he never got well," Judy said. ``It had nothing to do with me. I was not in Vietnam."

"Crazy that Goodyear was able to survive the horrors of Vietnam but not Judy Buenoano," Orange said. "He had no idea he was married to a sociopath. She had no respect for the fact that he had just put himself on the line for her and the country. All she saw were dollar signs."

Judy poisoned James with arsenic and waited almost a week after his death before cashing in his three life insurance policies. A few months later, an "accidental fire" burned down their Orlando home. Judy would receive another $90,000 in fire insurance.

She lost her husband and her home. But her purse was never fatter.
NO GRIEVING WIDOWS ALLOWED

Judy would waste no time finding another man. Despite having three kids in tow, she would find a new love in Bobby Joe Morris when she moved her family to Pensacola.

It was business as usual for Judy as she had a fat bank account courtesy of James Goodyear and a new beau in Bobby Joe. Eldest son Michael, however, was not doing well in school. He scored on the low end on IQ tests and was a behavioral problem. Judy would get him evaluated at a state hospital in 1974 and then sent Michael out to foster care where he would also receive psychiatric treatment.

Judy's new home would suffer another "accidental fire" and she collected money from the insurance. She then took Michael out of foster care and moved to Trinidad, Colorado with Bobby Joe and the rest of her children. Judy then changed her name from "Anna Schultz" to "Judias Morris".

FOUR YEARS MAX

Judy would date Bobby Joe for four years before deciding it was time to cut him loose.

Bobby Joe would start to suffer from the same mysterious illness as James Goodyear did years earlier as he complained of dizziness and vomiting. He would be admitted to San Rafael Hospital on January 4, 1978, but doctors would not be able to pinpoint what was wrong with him. He would be sent home to Judy's care two weeks later. Two days later, however, he would would pitch face-first into his dinner plate, unconscious. He would be rushed to the hospital, but Judy knew that her "medicine" had taken effect.

Five days later, Bobby Joe Morris would be dead. Doctors would chalk up his death to cardiac arrest and metabolic acidosis.

Judy would wait, just like she did after she killed James, before cashing in on Bobby Joe's life insurance.

Authorities were none the wiser.

But Bobby Joe's family suspected something fishy was going on. Back in 1974, Judy and Bobby Joe had been visiting Brewton, Alabama when a man from Florida was found dead in a motel room in that town. Police would find the man in the room after receiving an anonymous call. He was shot in the chest with a .22-caliber weapon and his throat was cut open.

Judy's connection to the crime? Bobby Joe's mother had overheard Judy telling her son about the murder.

"The sonofabitch shouldn't have come up here in the first place," Judy said. "If he came up here he was gonna die."

Bobby Joe had told his mother about the crime on his deathbed. She thought the confession could be attributed to his delirium, but Bobby Joe told her too many specifics to ignore.

"We should never had done that terrible thing," Bobby Joe mumbled to his mother. "Never should have done that to him."

She tipped off police but they would not be able to find any fingerprints inside the room and no bullet was recovered from the corpse. The case remained unsolved.

WHAT'S ONE MORE SURNAME?

On May 3rd, 1978, Judy would change her name again. This go around, she would change her last name to Buenoano, which in Spanish meant "good year." She stated that she meant it as a tribute to her husband James Goodyear and her Apache mother.

Things continued to go bad with Michael as he dropped out of high school in the tenth grade. With limited employment opportunities, he would join the army in June of 1979 and get assigned to Ft. Benning in Georgia after basic training. When he was on his way to his new post, he visited Judy in Pensacola.

Judy greeted her son with open arms. Then she began poisoning him.

By the time he reached Ft. Benning, he felt sick. Army physicians would find seven times the normal level of arsenic in his body.

They could do little to reverse the damage done. Six weeks after his arrival, the muscles in his arms and legs and deteriorated to the point where he was a paraplegic.

"Michael had no use of his legs," Orange said. "And he could not move his arms past his elbow. Again, Judy was a sociopath. It is unfathomable for a normal human being, a mother, to do this to her own child. Yet she did it to Michael. He was always an inconvenience to her but now that he had military insurance he could become an asset in death."

Judy would give Michael the short shrift while favoring James and Kimberly. Michael and James didn't get along well as clearly their mother favored the latter. Judy would hide Michael when people came over because she was ashamed of him. She would have a neighbor named Constance Lang watch over him when visitors arrived.

"Michael didn't fit the picture Judy wanted to present to the world," Orange said. "She wanted to be looked at like a woman of high status. She drove a Corvette and owned her own business. Michael was a slow-thinking kid. She didn't want anyone to see that."

The army didn't investigate the reasons behind Michael's inordinate levels of arsenic. Instead, they set him up with leg braces and a prosthetic device on one of his arms.

He would be discharged from active duty because of the medical disability.

But his mother saw dollar signs.

The day after his return home, Judy wasted no time. She organized a fishing trip with Michael, James, and daughter Kimberly. They would leave Kimberly ashore at the East River bridge while they went into the water with a two-seat canoe. A small folding lawn chair had been placed in the middle of the canoe for Michael who had was outfitted with a leg brace, a fishing reel, and a ski belt.

James would state that had fished for about two hours when they were reaching shore when a "snake fell into the canoe." He said that everyone panicked as the snake slithered around. The canoe hit a log and capsized.

James would claim to have been knocked out by the impact and would remember nothing until he came to inside an ambulance.

He would tell this version to the court but when he was talking to Army investigators, he made no mention of a snake.

"There is conjecture as to how much James was involved or much did he know," Orange said. "The statement given to the army investigators is different from what he would state later in court. The statement given to the army was a written statement and the handwriting didn't seem to match his own."

A man named Ricky Hicks saw the overturned canoe, an ice chest, and a plastic bag in the river. He also saw Judy and James.

"I lost the other boy," Judy said as Ricky approached them on the shore. "A snake had gotten into the canoe and I tried to hold the snake down with a paddle."

"Where is he?"

"It's no use," Judy said, waving him off.

Hicks said Judy appeared to be concerned about James then asked him for a beer. He then drove Judy's car to a nearby phone and called the county rescue squad.

The rescue team arrived and began looking for the missing Michael.

The canoe had not moved as there was barely a current. They would find Michael's body one-quarter of a mile upriver where the canoe had been rescued. The rescuers stated that it should not have been a problem to swim upstream, suggesting that Michael could have been saved.

Judy initially said that Michael had a life jacket on but later recanted and said that it was a ski belt.

There was no ski belt on Michael when he was found.

Judy would later state that after the canoe capsized, she saw James lying face down in the water. She swam over and cleared his air passage to resuscitate him. She looked around for Michael then was picked up by Ricky Hicks.

"Michael disappeared under water," Judy said. "I went to rescue James. I almost lost both of my sons that day. Mothers just don't murder their children. If I'd have lost both of them, I don't know what I would have done. They would have had to put me in a mental institution."

"Kimberly's boyfriend would later testify that Judy had killed Michael for the insurance money," Orange said. "The children knew about their mother but she had clearly brainwashed them into silence. She provided for them, she fed them. She knew what was best."

Telling the police that she was a "clinical physician", they bought her story of the boat capsizing. The army investigators did not buy her account. Not having any evidence, however, they would eventually pay her Michael's military life insurance ($20,000). Investigators got suspicious, however, when they found out that two civilian life policies were taken out on Michael. The applications on both policies look to have been forged.

Judy's former sister-in-law, Peggy Goeller, would call to inquire how she was doing. She would make no mention of Michael's death during her first call but on a second call she told Peggy that Michael had died "during Army maneuvers".

MOVING ON

Judy would demonstrate very little grief over Michael's death and she would not be charged with his murder. Foremost on her mind was finding another man and another big check.

She opened a beauty salon in Gulf Breeze and found her next mark: businessman John Gentry.

Gentry was more well-heeled than her previous conquests so Judy put on airs for his sake. She told him that she had Ph.D.'s in biochemistry and psychology and was the former head of nursing at West Florida Hospital.

Gentry believed her story and decided to spoil his blue-blooded girlfriend expensive gifts, vacations and the finest cuisine all in the name of courtship.

Pushing the envelope, Judy would encourage John to provide life insurance for both them both. She then secretly boosted Gentry's coverage from $50,000 to $500,000 without him knowing.

Two months later, Judy began giving Gentry "vitamin pills".

"Come on," she said, placing two pills into Gentry's palm.

"What are you, my mother?" Gentry asked.

"Well, God forbid I want to see you healthy," Judy slid the cup of water toward her prey.

Gentry would then complain of dizziness and later begin vomiting after his daily dose of Judy's "vitamins."

He would admit himself into the hospital and noticed that his symptoms disappeared when he stopped taking the vitamins.

Still smitten by Judy, he did not suspect her of wrongdoing. Instead, he took her vitamins and hid them in his briefcase.

One night, however, Judy sat him down for a special dinner. She had a very special announcement.

"I'm pregnant," she said, smiling in triumph.

"Finally," Gentry said. He told Judy that they should celebrate. She told him to go to the liquor store for an expensive bottle of champagne.

"Be right back," he said, kissing her with excitement.

Running out the door, Gentry got into his car and a bomb exploded with he turned the ignition key.

Amazingly, Gentry survived the blast as trauma surgeons saved his life.

"Judy really overplayed her hand with the explosion in the car," Orange said. "Really it speaks to her level of dedication and ingenuity. Who knows where she got the idea, maybe watching the Godfather. But the police found the dynamite residue inside Gentry's car. They decided to look no further than to Judy herself."

Their interrogation and research would unearth lie after lie. They found out about the $450,000 increase in Gentry's life insurance.

Gentry himself thought the insurance had been canceled. He was shocked to learn that she had increased the payout and was paying his premiums out of her own pocket. The police didn't spare him any quarter. They would him that she was not a real doctor and that she couldn't get pregnant.

"What?" Gentry muttered, completely flabbergasted.

Judy had been sterilized seven years earlier.

Gentry couldn't believe his ears. Police would go on to say that she had booked tickets for a world cruise for herself and her children...leaving Gentry out. They discovered that Judy had been telling her friends that Gentry was suffering from a "terminal illness."

The only "terminal illness" Gentry had was Judy Buenoano.

Now fully convinced, Gentry would reach into his briefcase and give police the "vitamin pills" that Judy had been giving him.

"Judy was emptying the vitamin casing and filling it with formaldehyde and a little arsenic," Orange said. "Over time, this would have been lethal."

The state attorney would refuse to charge Judy as they wanted an air tight case in order to prosecute. Knowing that they had their killer, officers, and federal agents searched Judy's home in Gulf Breeze, obtaining wire and tape from her bedroom that looked to match the same wire/tape they found on the bomb in Gentry's car.

They would search her son James' room, finding marijuana and a sawed-off shotgun. He would be jailed him for possession of drugs and an illegal weapon.

"Again, this is a strange mistake on Judy's part," Orange said. "She was meticulous and a good liar. Why she didn't remove any and all evidence from her home is a head-scratcher. She had gotten sloppy because she had gotten away with so many crimes before without so much as a slap on the wrist. She thought she was above the law, got careless and left incriminating evidence behind."

Judy would then be arrested at her beauty salon and charged with attempted murder. It took a month of police work, but authorities would trace the source of the dynamite used in the bomb, linking the Alabama buyer to Judy via phone records which showed numerous long-distance calls from her home.

Judy would pay bail but authorities would not let up. Five months later, she would be indicted for first-degree murder in the death of her son Michael, with an additional count of grand theft for the insurance scam.

Feeling the noose around her neck, Judy would fake a seizure and wind up in Santa Rosa Hospital.

Authorities then exhumed the bodies of the men they believed she killed. Bobby Joe Morris was exhumed with arsenic found in his remains. Identical results were obtained with the exhumation of James Goodyear, in the following month.

Connecting the dots, police obtained a court order to exhume the bodies of all the men that had died while associated with Judy; son Michael, husband James Goodyear, and boyfriend Bobby Joe Morris.

Arsenic would be found in all of the bodies.

"There was enough arsenic in him (Goodyear) to kill twelve people," Detective Ted Chamberlain said. "So he was loaded. I mean that boy was loaded with it when he went down."

OPEN AND SHUT CASE

In 1984, Judy would be convicted of the murders of Michael and attempted murder of Gentry. In a separate trial in 1985, she would be convicted of the murder of James Goodyear in which she would ultimately receive the death sentence.

Judy would be imprisoned in the Florida Department of Corrections Broward Correctional Institution death row for women.

HER FINAL HOURS

Judy would spend her last day watching a hunting and fishing show, eating chocolates, and talking about old times with her children and cousin Jeanne Eaton. She would read a suspense novel called "Remember Me" and her last meal with be steamed broccoli, asparagus, strawberries and hot tea.

Judy's impending execution did not receive the same media attention as Karla Faye Tucker whose was executed only a month earlier. Her execution was opposed by the Pope and Jesse Jackson.

'"She may not have been as photogenic, as young or as pretty as Karla, but she was just as good a Christian," Eaton said.

"Judy obviously had her enablers within her family," Orange said. "How could she be 'just as good a Christian' if she is poisoning people, blowing them up and the 'Christian' she is being compared to is ice-picking people to death. People say the strangest things."

But Judy herself was bitter that no one paid much attention to her presence on death row, particularly the fact that she was a woman.

``Karla was a young female, very attractive and she had become a Christian in prison," Judy said. ``We all prayed that she would be granted a stay of execution and clemency because we felt that she was a different person and she deserved a chance. Possibly, I am a different person. But I was a Christian when I came here. I was a devout Catholic. I've not changed in that."

"It was a bit of a curiosity as to why the media was so charged to prevent the execution of Karla Faye Tucker and paid little heed to Buenoano," Orange said. "Tucker's killings were ferocious and sadistic while Buenoano's killings could be seen as passive. But what drew people to Tucker was her physical appearance and demeanor. She came across as a sweet, reformed choir girl at the end. She had a charming smile and a soft voice. Buenoano, on the other hand, looked sinister. She had squinty eyes, high cheekbones and a snarling, Southern drawl. Her body language and demeanor screamed hostile."

Judy would enter the death chamber with several guards by her side. They strapped her into the large oak chair, placing leather straps over her waist, wrists, chest, and legs.

They fitted the calf and headpiece electrodes last, inserting a wet sponge in between to reduce the burning of Judy's skin.

"Do you have a final statement?" the warden asked.

"No, sir," Judy closed her eyes tight.

The witnesses on the other side of the glass partition watched in silence.

Judy did not look at them as a leather mask was placed over her face.

The warden nodded his head and the switch was pulled.

Steam wafted up from her right leg as her body jolted for thirty-eight seconds. Her hands balled into fists, white knuckling from the shock as smoke rose from her feet to the ceiling.

Then Judy went limp. She would be pronounced dead at 7:08 a.m., March 30th, 1998.

The date was her son Michael's 37th birthday.

SERIAL KILLING MOM : THE TRUE STORY OF JANIE LOU GIBBS

29

JANE CARLISLE

Janie Lou Hickox was born on December 25th, Christmas day, 1932 in Cordele, Georgia. Cordele is now a town with just over 11 000 residents, and is proudly known as the Watermelon Capital of the World. The city is named after Cordelia Hawkins who was the eldest daughter of Colonel Samuel Hawkins, the president of the Savannah, Americus and Montgomery Railway. In November of 1864, the area temporarily served as the capital of Georgia, but Cordele as it is now knows was founded in 1888 as a junction between two major railroads: the Savannah, Americus and Montgomery line and the Georgia Southern and Florida. Notable people from the area include jazz and blues singers, sportsmen, a White House Press Secretary and the president of an international Christian TV network. Nobody suspected that a serial killer who would be a black widow was growing up in their midst.

There is not much information about Janie's upbringing, but it was strictly religious and she grew up in a fairly poor family. Janie was married to Charles Clayton Gibbs, a farmer, when she was only fifteen. The two moved to the nearby town of Arabi which was just under ten miles away from Cordele, a mere fifteen minutes by car. Both of these towns fall under the Crisp County district. Arabi now has a population of 586, with 185 hosueholds and 125 families living in the town. Janie and Charles were regular churchgoers, and they had three boys: Roger Ludean Gibbs, Melvin Watess Gibbs, and Marvin Ronald Gibbs. For eighteen years, they lived quiet and devoted lives on the farm until tragedy began to take blow after blow upon the family.

Janie was known for spending all of her spare time helping out at the church and for her day-care service that she ran in her home for children of working mothers. Accounts note that on most days Janie would have around twenty-five children at her house aside from her own sons. While some believed her to have almost fanatic religious beliefs, all members of Janie's church and community believed her to be sound of mind and to know the difference between right and wrong, testimonies that they would later make in the investigation. Nobody felt that Janie had any emotional or mental issues, and simply knew her as a devoted mother who held God and the church close to her heart. When she wasn't looking after children in the community, Janie was helping out with events around the church and other ways to support the congregation.

Just before the tragedies began to occur, Janie had travelled to Albany, Georgia for a doctor's appointment. There she had been diagnosed with Lou Gehrig's disease, a motor neurone disease that destroys muscle control, is also known as amyotrophic lateral sclerosis or ALS. The disease progresses from a stiffness of muscles to twitching while the person becomes increasingly weaker. Eventually, once their muscles have decreased in size enough, the patient has trouble with speaking, swallowing, and eventually breathing. Janie was very aware that her body would begin to systematically shut itself down. After her trial, her defense lawyer Frank Martin stated that this was one of the most tragic aspects of the case as far as he was concerned. Frank believed that due to Janie's acute awareness of how her illness would progress paired with her fanatic religious beliefs, she wanted everybody that was close to her in the world to go to heaven so that she would be with them when she finally passed. Although Janie never admitted this in court, the murder of her husband, three sons, and grandson, all of whom she loved dearly, suggests that this might have been a contributing factor to the decisions or delirium that ended in her intentionally poisoning five members of her family.

The first member of the family to go was her husband, Charles Clayton Gibbs, who died on the 21st January 1966 when he was only thirty-nine years old. Janie was an avid cook, and she always had home cooked meals ready for her family when they returned home from work or school. After having had one such meal, Charles collapsed in the family home and was taken to hospital. Janie went to the hospital to care for him and brought a flask of soup with her. After Charles was served this final meal, he died painfully from stomach cramps and convulsions. Years later, investigators realized that this soup must have been laced with a particularly strong dose of arsenic from rat poison that Janie had been giving him in trace amount in his meals and coffees.

When administered in small amounts like this, it can be very difficult to determine if somebody is a victim of arsenic poisoning unless a doctor thinks to specifically check for it. Arsenic poisoning can result in a host of different symptoms and organ failures, so it is often the case that medical professionals are waiting for more evidence to be able to provide a solid diagnosis while the victim continues to be poisoned by somebody close to them. Symptoms can include abdominal pain and cramping, diarrhea, vomiting, dark urine, dehydration, vertigo, delirium, shock, hair loss, and convulsions. Arsenic is flavorless and odorless, making it very difficult for somebody to connect their normal food and beverage consumption with their illness. Arsenic poisoning can affect the skin, liver, lungs, and kidneys, which is both why it is such a potentially fatal condition and why it is difficult to detect without a hunch. In the case of Charles, his death was written down to an undiagnosed liver disease that he had been suffering for some time. While the doctors wanted to perform an autopsy on her husband to be sure, Janie said that she didn't want him 'all cut up', and her wishes were respected.

The church community provided an overwhelming amount of support for the Gibbs family once Charles had passed. The entire congregation was shocked, Charles having seemed to be in such good health until recent times, and also because he was still so young. The Gibbs family were provided with company, meals, emotional support, and everything that the members of their church community could possibly extend. When the life insurance claim for Charles came through, Janie donated a significant portion of these funds to the church to demonstrate her thanks for everything that they had done and her belief in the community. Janie claimed that she and the boys would have to continue on as best they could, and that she felt that with the strength of the church community behind them they would be able to make it through. Even after their home burned down soon after Charles' death and the family moved back to Janie's home town of Cordele, Janie continued to offer day-care services for the children of working mothers. There has never been an investigation into the house burning down, but the timing is certainly curious. Is it possible that Janie felt this was the only way to justify moving her family back to her home town of Cordele? It is clear from the rest of her actions over this two year period that she wasn't thinking rationally, and perhaps she wanted to escape the physical environment where she had been married for all of those years. Whatever the reason, just as nobody suspected that Janie had anything to do with the death of her husband, there was no investigation into whether or not the house burned down due to arson.

It was around this time that the oldest Gibbs son Roger took notice of a girl in their congregation, Ellen Penny. A relationship began to blossom between them under the watchful eye of Janie. The two teenagers began to spend more and more time together at church events, and participated in the same activities together. If Roger was assigned the duty of retrieving the bibles at the end of a ceremony, Ellen would always be there too help him. Very soon the two began to date. Over the next year Roger and Ellen married and she became pregnant with their first child. Ellen began living at the Gibb's residence, but this relationship and pregnancy was against a dark backdrop. It is difficult to say whether Janie took an immediate dislike to Ellen, or whether she did not want her son getting married and having a child so early like she had herself. Perhaps she wanted a different life for him, or harbored some resentment on being married off at such a young age. Either way, Janie never had a good relationship with Ellen and many times would behave as if she almost didn't register her existence.

Only months after Charles' death, Marvin began to develop the same symptoms as his father had. Having moved house and town, perhaps the rest of the family felt a separation with losing their father and like this wouldn't happen again with their youngest brother. There are no records of comments from the brothers or the community being concerned that Marvin would go the same way as his father, but sure enough, nine months after his father had died, Marvin Ronald Gibbs died on the 29th August 1966. Marvin too was determined to have an undiagnosed liver disease just like his father had, and Janie once again refused to have an autopsy performed. Perhaps Janie felt that performing an autopsy was an ungodly act that would in some way affect the chances of her family members getting into heaven? While the largest reason was most certainly to protect her own interests and for her to be able to complete her task, autopsy is a process rejected by many faiths and traditions. The police and staff at the insurance company pushed for autopsies as they felt that two deaths of this nature so close together and in one family didn't make sense. At this time, some members of the church community began to have suspicions about the deaths in the Gibbs family, but nobody wanted to be the one to come forward and accuse the pious and highly involved church member that Janie was. For many, there was still a huge disconnect. So even though the insurance company and the police of Crisp County were pressing for an autopsy on the body of young Marvin, Janie still had the support of the community enough to request that this procedure not be undertaken. Despite their suspicions, many in the community still felt that Janie wouldn't be capable of doing such a thing, particularly when it was to her own family that she seemed to have such an active devotion to.

Once again the church community poured support for the Gibb's family, offering counsel and companionship for Janie and her two remaining boys. When Marvin's life insurance came through, Janie once again provided a large portion of this claim to the church, which was undergoing significant renovations. While some began to talk about Janie seeming to almost be enjoying her new lifestyle, never being seen in the same dress and buying a new car, they could not help notice how generous she was also being with these funds. Those members of the community who still had faith in Janie chalked this spending down to a way to cope with her losses. However, Ellen Penny remained highly suspicious of Janie Gibbs. She didn't know how to speak out about her, both because she needed to live with the family and because she was so young, but after Marvin's death Ellen was certain that what was happening to the Gibbs family was no random or hereditary tragedy. Then, Melvin also began to fall ill.

As Melvin (often referred to in some articles as Lester) began to follow the path of his father and younger brother, the sixteen year old started to experience dizzy spells. Some people in the community attributed these headaches to puberty as the boy was sixteen. By this point, with such serious difficulties in the family, it is a wonder that Melvin's complaints weren't taken more seriously. He went downhill sharply. The doctors, not wanting to claim his death as another bout of undiagnosed liver disease that they weren't certain of, labeled his death a result of hepatitis. Once again a claim was made for life insurance, a portion donated to the church, and support lavished upon the Gibbs' family. At this point, Ellen became terrified for the life of her husband, herself, and their unborn child.

About a month after Melvin's death, Ellen and Roger's baby, Raymond, was born. Everybody noticed that Janie's mood lifted, and the community felt that this is where the horror ended for the Gibb's family. Janie was thrilled with her grandson, even though she had been so early married herself and her son had had his first child so early, making Janie a grandmother at thirty-four. Janie often used to show the baby to anybody who came around to the house, and would often be seen out with Raymond around the city. Ellen began to feel at ease around this time as Janie seemed to have changed entirely. The way that she interacted with Ellen seemed to have improved, and it seemed that the way that Janie went about all of her daily tasks with a different air.

However, even the baby began to fall ill soon. Ellen was in a state of desperation and didn't know what to do, the child only being one month old. The young girl has nobody that she could turn to, and didn't feel confident enough to make an accusation against Janie, even to her own husband. Despite the fact that Raymond was perfectly healthy, he died of an apparent heart condition. Everybody who was close to the Gibbs were completely shocked to hear of Raymond's death, and this is the point that many members of the congregation became highly suspicious of Janie. However, nobody did anything to prevent her from claiming the fifth and final member of her immediate family, her eldest and grieving son, with both Roger and Ellen still living with her at the time.

In the weeks after their baby died, Roger began to fall ill. Ellen, who was still under twenty at this age, had still not found the courage or the means to speak out against Janie. This may have been due to her living situation, or perhaps due to the sudden death of her son, but as Roger grew increasingly ill Ellen could do nothing but watch him deteriorate. She notes that during this time her husband constantly had red eyes, had visible rings around these, and was always pale and lacking in energy. He also used to get very severe headaches, but wasn't the type of person that liked to talk about any suffering that he was experiencing. The most that he would discuss these headaches was when he would be in such pain that he would be flinching. Ellen would ask if his head was giving him trouble again, to which he would respond with short and basic answers. Roger eventually found himself bedridden, being cared for by his mother. Despite what had happened to his father, two brothers, and own son, Roger never shared any suspicions about his mother with Ellen. It is entirely possible that he had figured out what was going on, being the last left, but didn't know how to get himself out of the situation.

Over the weeks, Roger's health got worse and worse. Ellen remembers overhearing an argument between Roger and his mother where he was repeatedly saying

"You did it! You did this to me!"

He was saying it over and over again as fiercely as he was able to in his deteriorated state. Ellen did not fully understand the conversation as she made sure that she kept out of sight. She asked Roger about it later in private, but he didn't reveal anything further and simply said that he and his mother had been squabbling over something. Ellen began to wonder whether she was paranoid about the situation, but it seemed that everything was pointing towards Janie's involvement in not only Roger's sickness but the suspicious deaths of the other four. Ellen stayed by her husband and cared for him as best she could, watching on as Janie nursed her son.

When Roger was eventually placed in hospital, Janie and Ellen spent nearly all of their time there. After a couple of days, Ellen noticed that Janie was in the habit of taking the water jug that the hospital placed in their room, tipping it down the sink, and replacing it with her own water. When Ellen asked her why she was doing this, Janie claimed that the hospital water had too much sulfur and that it hurt his throat. It was later realized that she was feeding her last remaining immediate family member increasing doses of arsenic through the water. Janie forced Roger to drink the water in large gulps and often. Once again, it is difficult to understand why this behavior was accepted by nurses, and also why nobody gave Roger testing for arsenic poisoning when four members of his family had died so suspiciously. However, even though this was a fairly common way for women to kill at the time, it is not until later years that we realized the signs and hints that might have saved the Gibbs family from their wife and mother.

One day, Janie asked Ellen to give Roger some water. Janie filled up a tall glass and placed it in Ellen's hand. Ellen gave Roger a small sip, but Janie demanded that he finish the whole glass, telling her that his throat is dry and he needs more. Ellen tipped the whole glass of water down her husband's throat, unknowingly giving him the final and strongest dose of arsenic. Perhaps Janie had been hoping that the blame might be placed on Ellen, or maybe she got satisfaction out of Ellen being the one that finally killed Roger, Janie having never been too keen on the girl. As Janie didn't want an autopsy on Roger, just like it was for the others, it is hard to say whether this act was a final insurance in her mind of her not being guilty of the crime, or whether it was the latter and she got satisfaction out of Ellen killing her spouse unintentionally. It is also possible, with Roger being left for last, that she was the least willing to kill him and needed Ellen to perform this final duty. After all, it would have made sense to kill the older two sons first and leave the younger one in her care, Marvin being so young and the least able of all three brothers to be able to take any action against his mother even if he had figured out what was happening. This suggests that Roger might have been somewhat of a favorite of Janie's, and that she wanted as much time with him as she could. Whatever the reason, Roger died soon after receiving the dose. He was only nineteen, and this finished Janie's work, whether it was insurance fraud or what she perceived to be God's work.

Just as she had with her two younger sons and her husband, Janie attempted to stop medical professionals from undertaking autopsies on Roger and Raymond Gibbs. However, as Ellen was the wife and mother, she has the rights of next of kin. Autopsies were performed that revealed extremely high levels of arsenic in Roger's organs, around twenty times that which you would expect to find in a body during an autopsy where arsenic has not been the cause of death. It was at this time that the Crisp County police called for the bodies of Charles, Marvin, and Melvin to be exhumed. People crowded around at the graveyard to watch while the bodies were taken out of the ground and placed on blue tarps. People began to say that they had thought there was something suspicious the whole time. A lot of guilt began to spread through the community. What if they had mentioned something earlier? Would they have at least been able to save the lives of Roger and his infant son? Mothers who had given their children to Janie to look after day in and day out felt embarrassed about their judgment of her character. This time the sympathy poured out for young Ellen who has lost her home, husband, and baby all within the space of a month. All five murders were committed in a short period of time, between 1966 and 1967. In all, Janie had received $31 000 in life insurance payments and given around ten percent of this to the church, but now she would have to answer for the crimes that she had done against those in the world that trusted her the most. Eric Hickey who has performed a study on female serial killers including Janie Lou Gibbs in 1991 claims that "These are the *quiet killers*, every bit as lethal as male serial murderers, but we are seldom aware of one in our midst because of their low visibility." Hickey also found that it takes an average of eight years to catch a female serial killer, nearly double what it takes on average to identify and arrest male serial killers.

Janie was arrested on Christmas Eve 1967, the day before her thirty-fifth birthday. She admitted to having killed all five of her immediate family members, but claimed that she didn't have a motive for doing so. While many people claim that she did this for the insurance money, there is still the chance that she genuinely committed the crimes in the name of her fanatic religious beliefs, wanting her family to be with her in heaven.

By February, Janie was determined to be insane and not fit for a trial but it was still agreed that she should not be able to live out her life in the community as she had been before. Janie took up residence at a state mental hospital where she served as a hospital cook, living there until 1976. At this time, multiple people had testified that they thought Janie was aware enough of her actions that she should have to deal with their legal ramifications. On May 9th 1976, Janie was convicted for her crimes and handed down five life sentences, one for each family member that she had poisoned. Janie's sister came to visit her in an attempt to understand the things that Janie has done, but found that she was largely nonresponsive and bewildered. The first question that her sister asked was *Why did you kill your family, Janie?* To which Janie responded she didn't know. Her sister attempted again, saying *Do you feel guilty?* Janice once again responded that she didn't know, seeming to be removed and numbed to the situation. Her sister made one final attempt to reach out to Janie and understand what had happened, asking *Can I do anything to help you?* For the third time, Janie responded that she didn't know. Her sister continued to visit her in jail in an attempt to understand more about Janie, what she had done, and what she was going through. But it seemed that no matter how much she tried, Janie was like a shell of what she had previously been.

She came up for parole seventeen times but was denied on each occasion. In April of 1999, due to her failing health as a result of Parkinson's disease, Janie was released into her sister's care. The last years of her life were spent in a wheel chair at a nursing home in Douglasville, Georgia, where she died on February 7th 2010. She now rests in the Sunrise Memorial Gardens at Lithia Springs in Douglas County, Georgia.

SERIAL KILLING MOM : THE TRUE STORY OF STACEY CASTOR

41

PAULA ANTHONY

Stacey Ruth Castor may have been one of the most sociopathic female serial killers in modern times. She poisoned her first husband Michael Wallace with anti-freeze after he becomes an inconvenience to her and did the same to her second husband David Castor years later. When she caught wind that the police were onto her methods, she poisoned her own daughter and wrote 'confession' letter on her behalf.

She tried to pin the crimes on her daughter.

Dubbed the Black Widow by the national media, recent findings have opened up the possibility that Stacey killed her own father as well.

Cool, calm and collected, Stacey maintained her innocence throughout the court proceedings, adamantly pointing the finger of blame at her own daughter. But what possessed her to kill not only her husbands but her own flesh and blood?

This is her story.

EARLY LIFE

Stacey was born July 27th, 1967 in Clay, New York. She would meet what she called the 'love of her life' in a bar at age seventeen.

His name was Michael Wallace.

"There was some kind of bet going on," Stacey's daughter, Ashley Wallace said. "He (Michael) had bet a friend that he would take her home that night. Then after that night they were together."

Stacey stated that she knew within the first five minutes of meeting Michael that she would marry him.

Michael was six years older than Stacey. He was loud and gregarious, always laughing and looking for a good time. This was a contrast to the personality of Stacey who was more withdrawn and kept people at arm's length. Michael brought her out of her shell.

"He was like something out of the 'Dukes of Hazzard'," Michael's brother-in-law Jonathon Corbett said. "He was all about yee-haw! Let's go have a beer. Just for fun. Let's go for a ride. Just for fun."

It would take five years for the couple to marry as they tied the knot at Stacey's parent's home.

Michael was a happy go lucky guy. But this happiness was fueled by drugs and alcohol according to Stacey.

"He had a problem with both for a long time in his life," Stacey recalled.

Michael would be arrested on numerous occasions for DUI. Finally, the judge got fed up and sent him to jail for a short period of time.

After he got out of jail, Michael vowed to change his ways. The couple married and Stacey would give birth to their first daughter, Ashley, in 1988.

"I knew from that minute on, my whole reason for being here was to take care of her," Stacey said.

Three years later, they would welcome another daughter, Bree.

Stacey would work as a dispatcher for an ambulance company while Michael worked nights as a mechanic. Times were hard financially but their contrast in personalities look to do them in. They would fight but it would not be about money because according to Stacey, "they had none."

PARENTAL FAVORITISM

Among their many disputes, Stacey would accuse Michael of favoring the youngest daughter Bree over everyone else. He would call Bree his "little princess" while paying less attention to Ashley. Stacey said that she made up for this perceived favoritism by becoming closer to Ashley.

"Bree was daddy's little angel," Stacey's friend Dani Colman said. "She could do no wrong. There was no talk of any relationship between Ashley and Michael Wallace."

The couple would continue to grow apart over the years and each was rumored to have had affairs. Still, their weakening marriage didn't seem to affect the children as both daughters remembered their childhood with a fondness.

"We'd just go for a ride in the car, you know?" Bree said. "For no reason, just take a ride. That was fun."

But by 1999, the couple were at odds on a daily basis. Suddenly, Michael began feeling sick. Over the holidays, his family members would describe him as having an unsteady gait and looking bloated. More than one person suggested that he see a doctor.

Michael would die in early 2000 with only eleven-year-old Ashley present in the room. She noticed he was sick but didn't think to call the doctor.

"He was laying on the couch, making what I thought were funny faces," Ashley said. "And all of sudden, he just sticks his arm up in the air and puts his arm on his side and then his arm just fell down."

Ashley left her father on the couch and went to pick up her sister Bree from school. "I've relived this day over and over again in my head, because what if there was something that I could've done?" Ashley recalled . "Like, I should've known, but I didn't. I was 11!"

Doctors would tell Stacey that Michael died of a heart attack. Michael's sister, however, held her suspicions about his demise.

"The color of his skin from head to chest was deep, dark purple," Michael's sister, Rosemary Corbett said. And it was really weird."

She wanted an autopsy but Stacey steadfastly refused.

"Stacey knew how to cover her tracks," forensic psychiatrist Paula Orange said. "Her mistakes came later in her serial killer career. And she was a serial killer, make no mistake about that. She didn't kill so much for profit or money. She killed out of convenience. When something wasn't going her way and she had to eliminate someone, she would do it without remorse or feeling."

THE GRIEVING PROCESS

Stacey took her two daughters and did her best to try and move on with their lives. She treated the girls to a trip to Disney World to try and put some happiness back in their life. Her gestures seemed empty to the children as she continued to hold things in and became colder to her children.

"My mom was never really around (after Michael died)," Ashley said. "I did all of the things she was supposed to do. I took care of my sister."

KILLING DAD

Stacey was also rumored to have been behind the murder of her father, Jerry Daniels, in February of 2002.

Michael's brother in law, John Corbett, found out that Daniels was hospitalized for a lung ailment. His condition was improving until his daughter Stacey visited.

Daniels would day soon after her visit and Corbett recalled Stacey giving him a can of soda for him to drink.

Stacey then had her father cremated and took control over his estate.

NEW HUSBAND

Stacey would start dating again, settling on David Castor. David was the polar opposite of Michael. He didn't party, didn't drink and had his own business. He had a stability that Stacey always wanted.

"He had money," Ashley said. "And my Mom was happy with that."

"He was attracted to Stacey because she accepted him," David Castor Jr said. "I think he just wanted someone there with him."

The new couple looked like peas in a pod. David had red hair just like Janice. He also had a thick, out of style mustache just like Michael Wallace before him. He looked like a scaled down version of Chicago Bear football coach Mike Ditka and had the fiery personality to match.

David had been married before to Janice Poissant. The two had a child together, David Jr, and had a happy marriage until David suffered a head injury during a motorcycle accident. He experienced amnesia for a long period of time and eventually got his memory back. His personality changed, however, and he would be a lot more brusque in his demeanor. He would soon prefer material goods over people. He would verbally abuse Janice until she finally decided to leave him after twenty-six years of marriage.

David had his own air conditioning installation and repair company which he purchased from Janice's father. His father-in-law had taught him everything about the business from the ground up. Janice and mother-in-law would work in the office while he went out on service calls. After his marriage to Janice ended, David's business began to flounder. His father-in-law bailed him out, however, and helped him put the business back on its feet.

Stacey would eventually replace Janice not only in marriage but in the business as well, becoming his office manager.

David didn't have Michael's substance abuse problems but he loved his toys. He would purchase motorcycles, jet skis, snowmobiles, and boats. His spending habits would cause a rift with his wife.

"They did fight because my Mom paid the majority of the bills," Ashley said. "And David just paid for his toys."

The marriage of blended families would cause a rift between the children. The girls did not take kindly to David's personality. He thought his controlling ways would keep the girls in line. Instead, his rules and regulations had the opposite effect.

The girls would rebel.

"At first, we didn't get along at all," Ashley said.

David had issues with the girls. He didn't allow his first wife an allowance and made it clear to the girls that he was the man "large and in charge."

Ashley would stand up to him first. She was older than Bree and had the bigger mouth. Stacey would intervene and do her best to try and make the girls see the positive benefit of living with David. They were closer to their school and had a bigger house.

The girls, however, had gotten used to being a threesome.

"David made it very clear that he didn't want any more kids," Bree recalled. "He didn't want to be our father and he didn't want to act like it."

He would send the teenage girls mixed signals, on one hand giving them the cold shoulder but on occasion trying to be their friend.

David and Ashley did eventually mend their ways as when she graduated from school she saw the 'proud father' look on his face.

"He wasn't trying to be like a Dad," Ashley recalled. "But like a friend."

"It is hard to tell what was going through David's mind when he married Stacey," Orange said. "He was probably one of those men who just couldn't stand to be alone. He would hold his step-daughters at arm's length but deep down it appears that he wanted their affection. He just didn't know how to reciprocate it."

MORE MARRIAGE TROUBLE

While David appeared to be building bridges with the girls, the gap between he and his wife was widening. They would fight on a regular basis until they had a huge argument on their anniversary weekend. David wanted to go away while Stacey had other plans.

She would claim they fought throughout the day and that David went to his bedroom and locked himself in. She then sent both of her daughters to go stay with friends while she went off by herself to leave David alone.

David didn't arrive at his workplace the next day and Stacey "thought something was wrong." She called the sheriff's department and told them that he had locked himself in the bedroom. He wasn't responding to her knocks at the door nor was he responding to her texts. She told authorities that he was "depressed" and "maybe suicidal."

Sheriffs arrived and kicked in the door of the bedroom only to find David lying dead in a pool of vomit.

Near his body was a container of anti-freeze and a half-empty glass of the green liquid.

"He's not dead," Stacey screamed as she saw his prone body. "He's not dead!"

Detectives would confiscate the evidence from the scene although it had the obvious look of a suicide.

With her husband declared dead, Stacey called her daughters on the phone.

"I have something bad to tell you," the crying mother said. "And I don't know how to tell you. 'Well, what?' David killed himself."

The coroner would state that David killed himself by drinking a lethal amount of the anti-freeze. But an alert investigator noticed a turkey baster in the garbage can outside the garage. He took the item as evidence and had it tested.

"Something didn't feel right to the investigators," Orange said. "Luckily one of them had a sixth sense about the situation. Something about Stacey seemed a bit off as did the so-called suicide itself. Men typically do not take the passive way out of drinking poison or sleeping pills. They most commonly commit suicide by blowing their brains out. David owned a shotgun. That remained untouched. Yet he chose to commit suicide by ingesting anti-freeze which would be a really painful way to go. Why suffer when you can have it over and done with a pull of the trigger."

The forensic analysis would reveal Stacey's fingerprints as the only ones on the glass on David's bedside table. They also discovered that the turkey baster at David's DNA at the tip.

"If the door was locked," Orange said. "Then how did the turkey baster end up in the garage with his DNA."

This evidence led them to believe that Stacey had "force fed" the anti-freeze to David who was too weak to fight back.

"She had drugged him asleep," Orange said. "If you near death or unconscious you are not going to notice someone dripping anti-freeze into your mouth."

Investigators began making inquiries among David's friends and family. They kept getting the same answer.

"David wouldn't commit suicide."

Authorities didn't play their hand just yet. They played dumb, allowing Stacey to believe she was in the clear. They wiretapped her house and listened in on her calls for any incriminating statements. They then set up cameras that monitored both her house and the graves of her husbands as Stacey had them buried side by side.

"You had Mike on the far left," Corbett said. "David on the far right. I said 'what's she doing, starting a collection up there?'"

"She had her name engraved on both of the headstones," Bree said. "It's kinda weird."

But Stacey would never visit the graveyard where her husbands were buried. She did call a friend but told the friend that she "didn't do any of it."

Investigators needed more proof and decided to have Michael's body exhumed. They ran tests on his body that would reveal that he had ingested the anti-freeze just like David.

Back at home, Stacey was oblivious to the investigation. She went about her days in a daze, ignoring her daughters.

"After David died," Ashley recalled. "It was just as before. She didn't want to do things with me and my sister."

COLLECTING CASH

Stacey would benefit from receiving David's estate. His own son felt shock and hurt when he find out he was left out of the will.

"Things had deteriorated between us after the divorce," David Jr said. "And it hurt."

It would later be revealed that Stacey had doctored David's will to exclude his son and give all proceeds of his estate to her. She had a friend who was a notary who later admitted to helping Stacey with forging the document.

Stacey would inherit the home and the air conditioning business which she quickly sold for a profit.

"There was so much sweat that went into that business," David Jr said. "My grandfather started that business. And she just threw it away."

Stacey would receive $200,000 free and clear.

KILLING ASHLEY

By September 2007, Stacey felt the noose tightening around her neck. She eventually found out about the police exhuming Michael's body and finding the lethal dose of anti-freeze that she administered. Then the sheriff's arrived at her door.

One of the sheriffs described Stacey as having the 'deer in the headlights' look as they approached. The normally cool and collected Stacey stammered during their interrogation and mistakenly referred to a news story wherein the wife had poisoned her husband using "anti-free".

One of the sheriffs noted that she used the word 'anti-free' as opposed to 'anti-freeze'. This would later prove to be a huge mistake on Stacey's part.

Stacey would return home and she desperately needed a way out. She needed someone to take the blame. A blood sacrifice.

Even it was her own daughter.

Police would arrive on Ashley's college campus (Bryant & Stratton) to question her about her father's death. It was Ashley's first day of school and they informed her that stepfather had been poisoned instead of having a heart attack.

Ashley became angry at the investigators. She was insulted that they would even think that her mother could kill her father.

"I didn't believe that she did it," Ashley said. "I never thought for a second that she would ever hurt anybody. They couldn't figure out why he killed himself. They were just trying to pin it on somebody else."

Ashley was in disbelief and called her mother. Stacey invited her home.

"You've been through enough," Stacey said. "Come home and let's get drunk."

Ashley agreed, still trusting her mother as her 'best friend.' She arrived home and Stacey gave her a 'nasty-tasting' drink. It was a mixture of Vodka and Sprite.

And unknown to Ashley, anti-freeze was added to the cocktail.

"Just keep stirring it," Stacey told her daughter who spat up the drink. "It has Sprite in it."

"All I remember was going to sleep at one o'clock on Thursday," Ashley recalled. "Then when I wake up it isn't Thursday anymore it's Friday."

Hours later, Ashley would be found in a coma-like state by her sister Bree. She screamed for her mother to call 911 before seeing a note beside Ashley.

"I found this note by Ashley's bed," Bree recalled. "And it said all of this stuff, 'Dear Mommy, I'm sorry. And it was typed. And I was like 'Oh my God, you have to see this.'"

Stacey knew exactly what was happening to her daughter. Yet she played the role of the distraught mother to the hilt.

"My daughter has taken some pills," Stacey choked back tears as she spoke to the dispatcher. "It sounds like there's something in her throat. Ashley. Oh my God. Oh my God. Oh my God."

Medics would rush to home and take Ashley to the hospital. They had discovered she had ingested a lethal dose of painkillers. Stacey had crushed pain medication pills and poured them in Ashley's drink, creating a lethal cocktail. Had the paramedics arrived only minutes later, Ashley would have been dead.

Stacey made sure that the "confession" letter made it to the hands of the paramedics. The typewritten letter was over a page long, single-spaced, with Ashley giving details and specifics as to why she killed both her father and stepfather. At the end of the confession, she pleads for her mother "to forgive her."

Stacey did not expect her daughter to make it through. To her surprise, her daughter was revived and quickly questioned by police.

"It was all blurry," Ashley said. "All I remember was a man in a red shirt yelling, 'What did you drink? What did you take? What did you write in that note?'"

"The last thing I remember was my Mom giving me a drink," Ashley said. "It was something she had never done before."

The police officer was adamant about asking Ashley if she wrote the suicide note.

"I didn't write any notes," Ashley said, appearing confused about the question.

Witnessing the entire exchange, Bree would be the one to break the news to Ashley.

Their mother had tried to kill her.

ARRESTED AT LAST

Authorities would spend over two years accumulating evidence against Stacey. In 2007, she would be arrested for degree murder in David's death and for attempting to murder Ashley as well as frame her for the killings of David and Michael.

Ashley would be brought to the stand and testify that she did not kill David or Michael. She also said that she did not type up the computer-generated "confession" letter where she revealed that she killed both men. Stacey made a mistake in that she had prepared numerous drafts of Ashley's "confession" later on her computer. The drafts had timestamps and had been written while Ashley was away at college, proving that she could not have written the letters.

There was also repeated use of the word "anti-free" throughout the letter. This phrasing echoed what she had said during her interrogation with police.

Mounting further evidence, prosecuting attorneys argued that David's "suicide" didn't make any sense because his fingerprints were not on the glass of anti-freeze they found by his side. They stated that he had been force-fed the poison through the turkey baster. Stacey argued otherwise, saying that David got the idea after watching a documentary on Lynn Turner, a woman who would murder her lovers by using the poison.

"He was depressed lot," Stacey said. "The business wasn't going well."

THE DEFENSE

Stacey's defense team began attacking Ashley. They wanted to prove that she was someone capable of murder, even at age eleven.

They began documenting how Michael showed favoritism to Bree and that Ashley killed him out of jealousy. Belaboring the point, they said that Ashley never got along with her stepfather David and killed him out of jealousy as well.

Stacey would then be called to the stand. She stated that she thought Ashley was mentally ill. The prosecuting team then went to work on Stacey, shouting out their questions in an accusatory manner. They asked why if Ashley was mentally ill she had not one shred of medical history to corroborate that allegation.

Then came the coup de grace. The prosecution team revealed to the jury that it was Stacey's fingerprints alone on the "confession" letter and not Ashley's. They had wiretapped the home and stated that there were 'typing sounds' throughout the day.

The sounds of Stacey typing up the fake 'confession' letter.

The jury deliberated for only two days before pronouncing Stacey guilty on February 5th, 2009 of second-degree murder in the death of David and attempted murder for overdosing Ashley with drugs and Vodka

The judge ordered her to serve a maximum of 25 years to life for the murder of David and another 25 for the attempt to kill Ashley. An additional 1 to 4 years was added for forging David's will.

Ashley still retained mixed feelings about her mother as it all came as a shock to her.

"I never knew what hate was until now," Ashley said. "Even though I do hate her, I still love her at the same time. That bothers me, it is so confusing. How can you hate someone and love them at the same time? I just wish that she would say sorry for everything she did, including all the lies. As horrible as it makes me feel, this is goodbye mom. As hard as you tried, I survived and I will survive because now I'm surrounded by people that love me. I'm going to do good things in this world despite making me in every sense of the word an orphan."

RANTINGS OF A SOCIOPATH

Stacey would be admitted into the Bedford Hills Correctional Facility for Women in Bedford Hills, New York.

Stacey would continue to place guilt on her daughter, Ashley. "She brought this on," Stacey said. "Bree was an innocent victim in all of this. I lost her, I lost my husbands."

"I was happy that they said she was guilty," Bree said. "Because we all know that she's guilty."

Ashley would be haunted by her mother's betrayal forever.

"I would have done anything for her," Ashley said. "But she tried to kill me instead."

DEATH

Stacey would be found dead in her cell on June 11th, 2016. Her cause of death remains under investigation.

HUSBAND KILLER : THE TRUE STORY OF MICHELLE HALL

55

TORI BAKER

It's never easy being a member of a blended family. There's a certain understanding that comes along with a second or third marriage – especially one involving children – that there is going to be a fundamental need for combined effort, tolerance and compromise.

When Michelle Garner remarried for what would be the third and last time, family and friends believed she had finally found happiness after reconnecting with an old high-school flame.

John Brittson "Britt" Hall, an aircraft mechanic and home builder, had known his own fair share of heartache; he was recently divorced when he found his old high school girlfriend, Michelle, on an online dating web site.

Britt Hall and Michelle Garner first met in 1986 while attending high school in Newnan, GA. The two briefly dated before Michelle Hall graduated in 1987.

"They both were in the popular clique," forensic psychologist Robert Brion said. "Britt was a baseball player that all of the girls had a crush on. Michelle was popular herself, very outgoing with a lot of friends."

The parents of Britt and Michelle were friends as well but they didn't consider the dating relationship between Michelle and Britt to be a serious one. After graduation, Michelle would move away and she would marry a man named Rusty Hart. The couple would have two daughters until their divorce in 1996.

The single mom worked as a dental assistant to support her daughters. Times were tight until 1999 when she met and married Steve Davis.

"Steve Davis was a businessman," Brion said. "He was divorced himself with a daughter of his own. He met Michelle and quickly fell for her charms as she could come across as a very warm and caring person. He asked her to marry him after about a year of dating."

Michelle would become pregnant during the union and give birth to her third daughter, Alyssa.

Unfortunately, her second marriage met the same fate as her first and within a few years, the couple had filed for divorce, citing irreconcilable differences.

Britt did well for himself after high school, becoming an airline mechanic for Delta Airlines. He made good money with Delta until they laid him off. He then went into business with his father in home construction until ultimately returning back to Delta after they had a rehire.

His marriage started to fail, however. His first wife cited that Britt had "mental problems" and filed for divorce, stating that the marriage was "irretrievably broken."

"Britt's first wife would take him to court at least six to eight times a year after their divorce," Brion said. "He was depressed and the court visits weren't helping."

His divorce would coincide with Michelle's impending divorce with Steve Davis. Her divorce with Davis was a particularly nasty one and Britt could sympathize. They would reconnect over a dating website.

In the midst of her own divorce, Garner was happy to find love again with Britt Hall as they rekindled old flames. Shortly after reconnecting, Britt invited Michelle over for Sunday lunch with his family, and all seemed well for the couple.

"Michelle did mention to Britt's family that she was going through some difficult times with her divorce," Brion said. "She was cheerful throughout but hinted that the custody battles she was going through were quite serious."

Little did Britt Hall's family know that their excitement would soon be turned to devastation; a tragedy that would make national headlines and be detailed in various murder documentaries.

THE BRADY BUNCH

Ronald Hall, Britt's father was all to happy to have Michelle back in his son's life. At least at first.

"We visited and talked," Ronald said. "And she came in and was just as happy as she ever was," he said.

It wasn't long before Britt Hall's romance with Garner turned more serious, and the two tied the knot in September of 2006. The new marriage was an adjustment, to say the least. Britt had three children from his previous marriage and Michelle Hall had three of her own children as well. The blended family of eight was now living in Britt Hall's town home.

"You can imagine how tight the living quarters were," Brion said. "But Michelle's girls really took to their new stepfather. They became comfortable enough to call him 'Dad.'"

Britt wanted a bigger home and decided to build a large home with the help of his father. The men paid for contractors to pour concrete and establish the foundation, but father and son built the majority of the house by hand.

"People didn't know where the couple were getting the money to build the house," Brion said. "But Britt did most of the work himself after the foundation was laid. So he was able to save a lot of money when it came to sweat equity. That's a testimony to how badly he wanted the marriage between he and Michelle to work out."

When all was said and done, Britt and Michelle Hall were the proud owners of a beautiful 4100 square foot home on ten acres, the perfect place to spend the rest of their lives together. The brand new house boasted vaulted ceilings, granite counter tops, and a finished basement. The construction would prove to be a house of cards, however, as things were brewing underneath the surface.

Michelle didn't have much luck with her two previous marriages, and although individual accounts may vary, her two former husbands are both to have reported being abused by Michelle during the course of their marriage.

Michelle never had a firm grasp on her emotions and didn't handle anger well. These character flaws would not bode well for her life with

Britt. Dealing with both partners' ex-spousal issues including custody and visitation, Michelle and Britt found themselves tinkering on the edge of divorce after a few months into their marriage.

"The way Britt and Michelle handled their issues were different," said family friend Sue Mathis. "Michelle was quicker to speak her mind and a lot of times, Britt just wanted her to try to gain a little bit more self-control."

Dealing with his own ex-wife and their similar divorce problems, Britt Hall was also facing his own internal battles with depression. Although he wasn't often the instigator in their frequent arguments, he was known to fervently engage in the verbal conflicts. While this certainly wasn't conducive to a happy and fruitful marriage, Britt Hall made it clear to friends he would not give up on his family and the life he had built.

The next couple of years came with continued stress, intensified by financial worries after the Halls realized they had gotten too far deep in debt as a result of building their dream home. Notices of foreclosure, liens on the house, and over-extensions were haunting the couple and causing both spouses to hit a breaking point.

On July 30, 2008, it was another typical tense day in the Hall household. Friends say Britt Hall, already aggravated due to a landscaper failing to complete a job on time, went to the store to pick-up hot dogs for a family get-together.

"Hey hon," Britt said as he called his wife. "How many hot dogs do you think I should get-"

"Count how many damn people are here," Michelle snapped. "That's how much you should get."

This would be the snide comeback that would break the straw in Britt's back. He grew tired at her constant bickering and baiting. When he came home that evening, a fight would ensue.

Michelle's youngest daughter, Alyssa, was in the living room watching television as her mother vacuumed to prepare for the company soon arriving. When Britt Hall told Alyssa to turn the TV down, another argument between the couple ensued and Hall immediately told her daughter to go upstairs to her bedroom and not come out until she was called.

There are only two individuals who know the details of what followed on that evening, and only one of them lived to tell. When all was said and done, Britt would be dead and Michelle would be charged with murder.

The 911 call came in at 8:02 p.m. by a frantic Michelle who told dispatchers that her husband had tried to kill her and commit suicide.

"He shot at me, and we were fighting to get it," Michelle told dispatchers regarding the weapon. She said she heard the gun go off twice. Seconds later, she told dispatchers her husband was turning blue.

When police arrived, Britt Hall was dead and had three noticeable gunshot wounds to his body: one on his left arm, one on his right thigh, and a close-range shot to his chest. Michelle Hall, bruised, scraped and covered in blood, told first responders the same story she had told dispatchers: her suicidal husband had tried to kill her before turning the gun on himself.

Prior to further investigation, deputies on the scene immediately called Britt Hall's parents and told them their son had committed suicide. The Halls refused to believe the news.

"Things just seemed to be going too good at this time in his life for him to have done that," said his mother, Charlene Hall. "I knew he didn't kill himself; I knew for a fact that didn't happen."

It didn't take long for police to begin seeing the crime scene a little differently than Michelle had described. Blood splatter and numerous bullet holes covered the downstairs bedroom, and a trail of blood led into the bathroom where Britt Hall's lifeless body now lay. If this was a suicide, there sure was a struggle beforehand.

Investigators gave Michelle the opportunity to explain the scene. She told how an argument between the couple turned violent when

Britt Hall threw her onto the bed. He immediately went into the study and she followed him.

Then she noticed the gun on the computer desk.

Knowing her husband was battling depression, she said she immediately became concerned with his safety, worried that he may use the gun to harm himself.

Michelle stated that she instinctively dove for the gun, and that's when Britt Hall reached for it as well and the two began struggling for possession.

After both Michelle and her husband lost control of he gun, she quickly picked up the weapon and began shooting rounds into the walls and floor in an effort to unload the gun.

In the hall, Britt Hall caught up with her and that's when she said he threatened to kill her. In yet another entanglement of an attempt for control of the gun, Michelle said the gun accidentally went off. This shot punctured Britt Hall's thigh, and that's when Hall claimed she went to call for help.

Britt Hall began crawling into the bathroom, unable to walk and calling out her name for help. When she approached him, gun in hand, she said he grabbed the pistol from her, put it to his chest, and pulled the trigger.

The problem with her story, however, was that most suicides don't entail multiple gunshot wounds. Additionally, the manner in which the fatal shot was delivered raised eyebrows for investigators.

"I've worked many suicides in my career, and I've never worked a suicide that I can remember where a man had shot himself in the chest," Lt John Lewis said.

Furthermore, the gunshot wound on Britt Hall's chest had no signs of charring or burning around the entry wound, signs which usually indicate a self-inflicted wound.

Britt Hall also had a shattered elbow and a bullet hole in his left arm. Three different shots, all which led investigators to believe they weren't being told the whole story.

Michelle did her best to persuade the investigative team to believe her story, but her story changed upon being brought to the station for questioning. While at first she claimed the two struggled for control over the gun, she then claimed Britt Hall was never actually in possession of the gun at all.

Coupled with the evidence at the crime scene and her story's inconsistencies, Michelle was charged the next morning with the murder of her husband.

Crucial to the prosecution's case was the testimony of Michelle's youngest daughter, Alyssa, who was in the home during the shooting. Police brought the 8-year-old in for questioning immediately following the incident and she clearly stated she heard her step-father pleading with her mother to "put the gun down," she said. Alyssa would ultimately testify in her mother's trial in 2009.

Facing charges of malice murder and aggravated assault, Michelle vehemently denied killing her husband. She insisted that he died of a self-inflicted gunshot wound after threatening suicide and fighting with her over the .38 caliber revolver.

The fight that evening was par for the course, she said. The two regularly got into verbal and physical altercations, and their marriage was falling apart due to financial stress. They would also constantly fight over ex-spouses, custody and visitation regarding the six children. Although there were no police reports relating to any domestic altercations in the home before, family and friends knew things weren't okay on the home front.

"Britt would spend several nights driving to work calling me and saying 'I don't know what to do.' He would have done everything in his power to save his marriage, even if it was not worth saving. He was terrified of failure," said Mathis.

One of the first fights that turned physical in front of the family was in November 2006, when Britt Hall's eldest daughter came into the room to find Michelle Hall unconscious. Her father quickly ushered her out of the room and told her not to worry about it. The next couple of years only brought more trouble due to the same old problems and Britt's alleged mental illness.

Britt was prescribed three different types of medication for depression at the time of his death, police confirmed.

But the physical evidence did not add up to suicide. Initially, the Georgia Bureau of Investigation estimated the fatal gunshot to have been fired from around 18-24 inches away. This is not consistent with suicide, detectives argued. While many victims of mental illness fall prey to suicide each year, the facts must add up. In this case, they did not.

If convicted, Michelle was facing life in prison.

In September of 2009, testimonies were heard by Alyssa Davis, as well as responding officers Capt. Tony Grant and Sgt. Freddy Cox, about what they saw and heard on the night of the shooting.

Cox testified that Hall's appearance was "consistent with someone who'd been in a physical altercation" and that Hall had bruises, scrapes and blood on her neck and forehead as well as blood on her hands and a knot on her elbow.

During his testimony, Grant stated he immediately noticed that Hall's face was red and she had what appeared to be gun-shot residue on her hand, even though she was stating her husband had committed suicide.

There were multiple bullet holes throughout the downstairs of the home when police arrived on the scene, Grant testified. Two bullets were recovered from Britt Hall's body and three more were found in the house.

Grant said a blood pattern analysis showed blood spatters of 90 degrees in the downstairs quarters outside of the bathroom, proof that Britt Hall crawled into the bathroom after being wounded.

Defense Attorney Mike Kam said that while in no uncertain terms would he call the key ear witness a liar, her age and her location during the shooting did not make for the most reliable testimony.

"She was eight; she didn't see anything, she clearly got some of the facts confused." Kam said in an interview. "She's not someone who is used to being asked questions in formal interview settings. Who knows what she remembered, or what happened?"

Additionally, Kam indicated that Michelle certainly didn't fit the description of a murderer. Outside of two divorces, Hall had no criminal record. She was law-abiding citizen, with nothing in her background which would give the assumption she was capable of murder, he said.

But the jury had heard enough. On September 25, 2009, Michelle Hall was found guilty on all counts in the death of her husband Britt.

Not long after her conviction, Hall's attorneys filed a motion for a new trial, citing trial court errors. Coweta County Superior Court Judge Jack Kirby denied the motion and the defense attorneys took the case to the Supreme Court.

On September 22, 2010, the Supreme Court of Georgia upheld the conviction, despite Hall's defense's argument that the trial court erred by admitting similar transaction evidence and prior consistent statements.

Hall's defense stated that testimony from both of her ex-husbands that she was verbally and physically abusive were inadmissible because they were not "sufficiently similar" to establish proof of the crimes for which she was charged, according to the opinion of the Supreme Court. It also stated that "in cases of domestic violence, prior incidents of abuse against family members or sexual partners are more generally permitted because there is a logical connection between violent acts against two different persons with whom the accused had a similar emotional or intimate attachment."

The opinion also added that the fifteen and thirteen-year lapses of time between her ex-husband's allegations of abuse to the alleged shooting of her husband did not require exclusion of evidence.

"Given that the similar transaction evidence reflects appellant's behavior towards prior spouses, we conclude that any prejudice from the age of these prior incidents was outweighed by the probative value of the evidence under the particular facts of this case and the purpose for which the similar transactions were offered."

Eighteen months later, however, Michelle retained a new attorney who filed a habeas corpus petition, stating Michelle was given ineffective legal counsel by Kam during her trial in 2009. Senior Judge Robert B. Struble presided over the hearing and determined that Hall was in-fact entitled to a new trial. Struble agreed that Kam, Hall's trial attorney, was "ineffective and fell below the minimum guarantee of representation under the constitution," a press release said.

While Michelle may have been looking forward to another chance at redemption, The Attorney General's Office quickly announced their plans to appeal the habeas corpus ruling to the Georgia Supreme Court.

In a press release on March 30, 2012, Coweta County District Attorney Peter John Skandalakis expressed his respectful disapproval of the court's ruling and that in stating Kam was ineffective for representation, "the court erroneously applied the wrong standard under the law."

Skandalakis said he was optimistic that the Supreme Court will conclude that Hall had a legally sufficient defense and that her conviction would be upheld after review of the appeal.

On January 22, 2013, the Supreme Court found Hall's convictions to be fair and just, denying insufficient representation during her 2009 trial. According to the court summary, the Supreme Court concluded that the habeas corpus petition did not conduct proper legal analysis to determine the effectiveness of Hall's defense.

The opinion references Strickland v. Washington, a 1984 Supreme Court case in which it determined that to be granted a new trial, a defendant must show that it was due to insufficient performance by defense that the defendant was found guilty.

Michelle's argument for her habeas corpus petition was that "if she were in the same room when her young daughter was questioned, she could have assisted her attorney by prompting him with specific information," the court says in its opinion. However, it was determined during the habeas hearing that any information she would have portrayed to her attorney was already known information to both parties. "As such, Hall has failed to show actual prejudice, and her claim of ineffective assistance of counsel should have been rejected," the opinion said.

Today, Michelle Hall remains in a Coweta County prison.

Since her conviction, Michelle's ex-husbands have been given full custody of her three respective daughters.

She won't be eligible for parole until 2039. She will be 70 years old.

MARCIA KELLY

The morning of October 23, 2005, seemed to start much the same way as any other morning in the sleepy town of Cushing, Texas. Marcia Kelly, a 35-year-old mother of three, was wrapping up a grueling night shift at the nearby hospital where she was employed. As the sun began to rise, she made a phone call to her stepfather-in-law, David Bone. Marcia explained to the older man, still drowsy from a sound sleep, that she had been trying to send a "wake-up call" to her husband, James Kelly, with little success. A trucker by profession, James had spent the previous evening "off" deep in routine maintenance of the automobiles that supplied his livelihood – having finally retired at around 2 am, he had requested that his wife rouse him early the next morning via a telephone call in order to get a head start on the upcoming day's tasks. Bone's household stood just a few hundred yards from his stepson's property, so he had no obligations to fulfilling Marcia's request to check on James in person.

Friendly with the family and familiar with the humdrum routine of everyday life in Cushing, Bone suspected nothing amiss when he walked through the door of the Kelly residence. But upon reaching James' bedroom, he suddenly became hesitant. Nothing seemed particularly out of place aside from a cell phone, which lay open on the floor as if it were waiting for somebody to use it. The figure of a man was clearly visible beneath the sheets of the bed, but Bone found its stillness to be unsettling. After a minute or so of not being able to wake up the bed's occupant with the butt end of his walking stick, David mustered up his courage and pulled away the quilt covering up the body. What he found underneath was something truly horrific. The lifeless corpse of James Kelly laid stiff beneath the blankets, surrounded by a pool of blood draining from a single bullet lodged deep into his skull.

Immediately, Bone called 911, though he knew it was far too late for his son to be saved by even the most skilled doctors. Once the ambulances and investigators sounded their sirens and rushed to the scene, it was up to him to notify Marcia as to why her husband would not return her calls. Utterly shocked, she clocked out of work and rushed straight to the crime scene she had once called home. Only upon her arrival would the Kelly family's nightmare be fully realized. Amongst whispers shared between curious neighbors gathering around the flashing lights and barricade tape, the identity of the sole suspect in the brutal murder became crystal clear – Shaina Sepulvado, Marcia's eldest teenage daughter.

* * *

Fourteen years earlier, James and Marcia met eyes for the very first time. Friends often described him as a "good old boy" – the charismatic 19 year old was constantly seeking out adventure, despite the fact that it often landed him in trouble. Although Marcia was only two years his senior, she had already made her way down a much darker path. After dropping out of high school in the ninth grade, she began hanging out with the rowdy crowd of petty criminals. Between the ages of 17 and 21, she had been married (and divorced) twice. The two marriages subsequently produced two healthy daughters. However, motherhood did very little to tame Marcia, who continued to frequent the party circuit filled with drug abuse and drag racing. Concerned with little outside of having a good time, the two soon crossed paths and became instantaneously attracted to one another. On the surface, the feisty girl who wasn't afraid to get down and dirty seemed to be the perfect fit for him. For the next several years, the two casually dated on and off. Neither made fidelity a priority in the relationship; over their first few years together, James had two sons with another woman, while Marcia gave birth to a third daughter by a different man. Ultimately, their non-committal attitudes likely kept their relationship together through the affairs. Regardless of everything that happened, the two had a mutual understanding of one another and always managed to find their way back into each other's arms.

Unfortunately, circumstances finally came about that forced the pair to grow up and leave behind the wild lifestyles of their past. In 1995, James was convicted of violating probation and was promptly sent to prison. Just a few months later, a tragic fire destroyed many of the family's possessions and stole the lives of Marcia's mother and middle daughter, Kaitlyn. Though the eldest and youngest daughters were spared from the flames, the surviving children did not escape unscathed. Shaina, just 6 years old at the time of the incident, fell into a deep depression following the loss. At the height of her grief, the little girl attempted suicide by riding her bicycle straight into the path of an eighteen-wheeler barrelling down the road outside of the family's home. Although she escaped unharmed, Shaina was sent to the hospital for a psychiatric evaluation and remained there for several months to receive treatment. Shaina would never truly recover from the trauma – following the suicide attempt, she became aloof and defiant; "a child that pushed people away," as Marcia described it.

More often than not, these types of unfortunate events split relationships apart at the seams. The opposite held true for Marcia and James. With the time and distance to think about their past decisions, both became incredibly motivated to turn their lives around for the better – together. While James sat behind bars, the two began writing letters to one another in which they'd discuss their plans for the future. After years of fun and games, the two had grown to become each other's support system.

When he was finally released from the county jail, James immediately began saving his money. He eventually invested in a big rig truck, and after many long hours and thousands of miles logged, James began to reap the fruits of his labor. He hired several employees and two more trucks, transforming himself from an independent driver to the head of his own small firm by the time he reached his 30's. While her partner worked behind the wheel, Marcia found the drive to put herself back in school. After studying respiratory therapy, she was able to find steady work in her local hospital. She further capitalized upon her earnings through a self-launched bounce house rental service on the weekends. With a great deal of hard work, the blue-collar couple quickly began to climb the rungs towards a middle-class lifestyle. As their financial pursuits blossomed, so too did their romance. Marcia and her daughters shared a home with James and his sons when the two finally decided to get married. Although she was content with a simple courthouse ceremony after the failed relationships of her past, James insisted they properly proclaim their love in front of family, friends, and God in a traditional chapel wedding. On Valentine's Day 2003, they celebrated much more than their union – the Kelly family used the opportunity to rejoice over the positive changes they had made and the seemingly bright future that lie ahead of them.

From an outsider's perspective, their story sounds like a whimsical, idealistic, all-American fairy tale. Beneath the surface, however, tensions quickly began to boil over and dreams for the future began to dissipate.

One distinctive characteristic that set the Kelly's apart from the average family was their capacity to fight with one another. Whether the adults became quick to anger with the stresses they adopted or one or both of them had a propensity for meanness stitched into their DNA remains a mystery. Regardless of the reasons behind their temper, husband and wife were well known for their volatile screaming matches. Often times, the eager to please James would have to satiate Marcia by purchasing expensive gifts or automobiles. Unfortunately, the fighting branched out beyond the two parents. Shaina, aged 14 at the time of the marriage, was less than ecstatic about the new life she was being forced to lead. With a new stepfather as well as two step brothers living underneath her roof, her behavior shifted from rebellious to completely out of control, and at times, violent. Taking a step out of her mother's handbook, she became involved with the wrong crowd that frequently found themselves in trouble. Naturally, her parents became concerned. Unfortunately, that concern drove a wedge between the newlyweds instead of bringing the two together. Marcia firmly believed that the best solution to deal with her daughter was to allow Shaina the space and freedom to make mistakes – eventually, she'd grow tired of a wild lifestyle and settle down, just as Marcia had done. She didn't question whether her daughter attended school, or where she might disappear to on the weekends.

James saw things much differently. Anxious to be a father figure to his new stepdaughter, he believed that discipline, boundaries, and stern rules were desperately needed to keep Shaina from danger. The discord in the family pushed the teenager towards moving out to a boyfriend's house, adding fuel to the heated arguments between stepdaughter and father. Frequently, Shaina would spit venomous threats concerning her desire to kill James. Meanwhile, Marcia and James would continuously argue over what the right course of action was for their child. The situation finally came to a head when Shaina returned home after the inevitable break up with her live-in boyfriend. Shortly after being forced under her parent's roof, she willfully refused to clean a messy room. What should have been a fleeting tantrum instead escalated into a physical altercation; after assaulting her own mother, authorities arrived and placed Shaina under juvenile probation. Her punishment proved to be not very effective. Rowdy as ever, the teenager soon began dating a 23-year-old sex offender by the name of Dallas Christian. The young lovers eloped in favor of a life of partying and riding without rules, much to the displeasure of James Kelly.

Despite his best intentions, James should have been relieved by the absence of his stepdaughter. She would soon prove to be the person responsible for his untimely demise.

* * *

In the heart of East Texas, just over 600 people call the former railroad town of Cushing their home. As is the case with many of the tiny, close-knit communities scattered throughout rural America, word travels at an incredible speed. Needless to say, word of James Kelly's murder reached a good portion of the townspeople within just a few hours of the event. Though the details surrounding the crime were hazy at best, rumors surrounding Shaina and James' troubled relationship flew out of the lips of neighbors. Although no one wanted to believe that such an atrocity could have happened in Cushing, everyone was able to come to a consensus and agree that Kelly had one (and only one) true enemy in all of Nacogdoches county – his own stepdaughter. It seemed that she was the only one who could have committed the crime so effortlessly. However, close family friend Kevin Dill was among the first to direct his suspicions toward a less likely suspect.

As one would expect from the spouse of a recent murder victim, Marcia was anxious to abandon her shift at Lufkin Memorial Hospital upon receiving the grim news from David Bone. Also typical of a person who has just experienced a devastating emotional blow, Marcia found herself too distraught to drive herself home. Instead, she requested that Kevin Dill pick her up and escort her to the horror that awaited her upon her arrival. As fast as he possibly could, Dill picked up the wife of his best friend. The two proceeded to drive down an empty country road at over 90 miles per hour, only to be stopped by a patrolling sheriff. Sobbing, Marcia hysterically explained the situation to the officer and successfully evaded a speeding ticket. However, shortly before approaching the Kelly household, Dill was startled by Marcia's sudden change in demeanor. Witnesses described her as "flat" and void of emotion. While bystanders wrote her demeanor off as the result of severe shock, Dill was startled by the direct contrast to the display she had put on moments before. After asking if the news of her husband's death was true, Dill recounted another instance of bizarre behavior. Rather than mourn her husband or ask to see the body of the man she supposedly loved, Marcia immediately became concerned with whether the family dogs had been fed breakfast. Amidst questions and concerns from authorities and neighbors alike, she retreated into the house and filled their bowls with food. Though Dill himself was in shock from the sudden death of his friend, he struggled not to attach meaning to Marcia's actions.

Suspicions aside, it immediately became clear that the murder had been intentionally planned out and executed based on a surface investigation. Nothing seemed to be particularly out of place or disheveled inside of the house, and with all of the family's valuables intact, the possibility of a robbery gone wrong was quickly ruled out. In fact, former Nacogdoches county sheriff Thomas Kerss described the scene as "serene". From the available evidence, it seemed as though the murderer strolled through the front door, shot Kelly, and left as if nothing had happened. Marcia firmly denied that anyone, in particular, held a grudge against James when asked about possible enemies. However, the fingers pointed toward Shaina and the men she surrounded herself with were not purely based on conjecture. Aside from the obvious animosity within the family, the group of teenagers were notorious for their erratic and unruly behavior around town fueled by drugs and alcohol. Further backing up the theory was the simple fact that Shaina Sepulvado, Dallas Christian, and Colton Weir (a juvenile who had found himself in and out of trouble with the law over the years) were conspicuously not present among the growing crowd of townspeople clamoring for more information. Certain that the trio must somehow be involved with the crime, police promptly tracked down Christian, Weir, and Sepulvado and arrested them in connection with the grisly murder.

At the initial interrogation, all three maintained their innocence. However, their guilt became apparent as inconsistencies began to take form in each of their stories. The teens claimed to have spent the night shooting guns by the banks of the Shawnee River, a popular hotspot for underage drinking and teenage debauchery. After not getting much out of Sepulvado and Christian, interrogators focused their efforts towards cracking the youngest of the trio, who seemed to be plagued with a guilty conscious. It didn't take much pressure to produce results – on the verge of tears, Colton Weir confessed to being the one to pull the trigger of the rifle that killed James Kelly.

* * *

For Colton, Shaina, and Dallas, partying wasn't so much an undesirable habit as much as it was a way of life. The teens tested positive for cocaine and methamphetamines, which they claimed to have used all day, every day while "riding the roads". On the 23rd of October, the three had been binging on drugs and alcohol and did, in fact, end up drinking down by the river as the night began to wind down. While inebriated, they discussed plans they had made previously to kill James Kelly. They had been talking about the possibility of committing the crime for some time, but had always held off, waiting for a more opportune moment – that is, until that drunken autumn night. Filled with adrenaline and far beyond clear thinking, the three agreed that the time had finally come.They proceeded to drive towards their prey through winding wooded roads, and upon their arrival, ceremoniously fetched gloves and a hunting rifle Weir had borrowed from a friend.

Quietly, Shaina led Colton into the house and directed him toward the room her father slept in. She then returned to the safety of the car, where Dallas Christian waited behind the wheel. Creeping through the darkness, Colton entered the bedroom to find James sleeping soundly after a long day's work on his mechanics. Just 10 feet away from the victim, he lifted his weapon and shot just once. The bullet made impact just above James' cheek, killing him instantly. The blood spattered teen returned to his friends outside, and together they made their way back to the riverbank. After tossing the gun into the water, they proceeded to burn several pieces of incriminating evidence.

The admission didn't come as a surprise to anyone – not only did the details add up to what authorities had found, it was eventually revealed that Colton had confided the murder plot to a number of townspeople ahead of time. Later on, investigators were able to use Colton's account to retrieve the rifle and damaged evidence almost effortlessly. When informed of their friend's confession, both Dallas Christian and Shaina saw the futility in lying about what they had done and dropped the charade of innocence. However, one thing remained uncertain to investigators. While Shaina's motive was crystal clear, it was hard to understand why the two men would get themselves involved in a serious crime against a man they hardly knew.

The answers Colton and Dallas had to offer caught the police completely off guard. Rather than pegging responsibility for the crime on Shaina's charm or ability to manipulate, the two young men instead placed their blame on a different person entirely – Shaina's mother, Marcia.

* * *

"Marcia had a desire to be 18 again," stated Lead District Attorney John Heath in an interview several years after the murder. It was no secret to anyone that the Kelly's marriage was far from picture perfect. However, unbeknownst to many of the residents of Cushing, Marcia had not completely given up her past. She continued to use drugs and alcohol frequently, and while her husband was on the road, she allegedly struck up sexual affairs with the neighbors. It was on these men that she first began toying around with the idea of getting rid of her husband permanently. What began in jest would soon become deadly serious, and after the murder, several men confessed that Marcia had offered them cash rewards for the life of James Kelly. Many refused to be involved outright, and Marcia would move on in search of a better foot soldier. Eventually, she found the pawns she was seeking in the young men her daughter surrounded herself with.

Nacogdoches, Texas was recently recognized as one of the poorest cities in the United States. With the median household income in Cushing falling well below that of Nacogdoches, many of the people in the tiny East Texas town had come to not expect much out of life. Born into unlucky circumstances, the boys Shaina spent her time with came from working class families struggling to get by. Marcia, on the other hand, was beginning to work her way out of generations of financial ruin. Unlike many of Cushing's residents, she was able to promise cash rewards, brand new trucks, and jet skis – luxuries the boys could only dream of. In addition to the monetary incentive, both Colton and Dallas were close to Shaina. Having heard countless stories of his rough, brutish nature, the boys were convinced that James Kelly was a violent, controlling man that deserved to be punished. Between the pleas of mother and daughter, the prospect of murder not only seemed like the morally right thing to do, it also seemed to be advantageous in the long run.

As it turned out, Marcia Kelly's motives for organizing the crime weren't far off from those of the teenagers she masterfully manipulated. The marriage was disintegrating because of the constant arguments and the fundamental disagreements over how to raise their children. Although

Marcia was willing to give up on the marriage, she wasn't willing to give up the financial stability that came with the marriage. Hatred or an escape from a toxic relationship didn't fuel the crime; instead, greed served as the driving force behind the actions. A quick look at Marcia's background and personal finances revealed that she had recently filed a $100,000 life insurance policy on her husband. A funeral director later remarked that she had asked several questions regarding cashing in on the insurance as they made arrangements for James' funeral, striking him as extremely cold and callous. In addition, Marcia was set to inherit nearly all of the assets from her husband's lucrative trucking business. If all went well, she would be wealthy for the rest of her life once her husband took his final breath.

Ever since Marcia's failure to inform the police of the tumultuous relationship her daughter and husband shared, police had been skeptical. When initially confronted about the possibility of her daughter being a culprit in the murder, she claimed that she had written off the threats Shaina had posed as the ranting and raving of any teenage girl. Initially, investigators had simply questioned whether Marcia might be covering for her guilty daughter. However, nobody had considered that she was the mind behind an elaborate murder for hire plot. Evidently, Marcia was confident that the authorities would not catch on to her – so much so that she had already spent hours at the police station of her own volition, claiming to be offering her daughter emotional support throughout her interrogation.

Friends, family, and neighbors were fooled as she played the part of conflicted mother and grieving widow well. Deflecting any suspicion with ease, members of the community offered condolences and helping hands, completely unaware of Marcia's guilt. On the day of James Kelly's viewing, the ceremony was interrupted by officers seeking out Mrs. Kelly. While mourners clad in black surrounded the body of the murder victim, police escorted the surprised Marcia Kelly back to the station for further questioning. She initially cooperated with authorities but quickly grew annoyed by the prospect of missing her husband's funeral. Before she could ask to turn back around to the procession, it was too late. She was presented with a warrant for her arrest and promptly taken into custody. Horrified, she plead for her freedom as she was locked away.

* * *

Nearly a year passed between Marcia's arrest and the beginning of her trial in the summer of 2006. As expected, she claimed her innocence in front of a jury of East Texans, hoping for the utmost sympathy. Unfortunately for her, Colton Weir, Dallas Christian, and several other men opted to take the stand to testify against her. The prosecution proceeded to bring to light the insurance policy and history of violence, cementing Marcia's untrustworthiness as a defendant. The mounting evidence certainly built a convincing case against her; however, none of it was able to conclusively link Marcia to the crime. Luckily, the prosecutors had a secret advantage to bring the case to a close.

The night shift at Lufkin Memorial Hospital was a strong enough alibi to place Marcia far from the scene of the crime on the night of the murder. However, during Colton Weir's confession, he admitted to investigators that Shaina had been in constant communication with Marcia throughout the night of the murder. With that sort of reasonable cause for suspicion, the courts were able to subpoena both mother and daughter's phone records. They revealed that there had in fact been a series of phone calls between the women during the window of time that the murder could have occurred. One call took place just moments after the estimated time of death; Shaina later reminisced that her mother had simply asked, "Is it done?" In addition, Marcia's phone records revealed that she had been in close contact with James leading up to the murder. Prosecutors speculated that these calls were made in order to get an idea of the victim's plans for the night, including when he might be headed for bed. As Marcia collected information regarding her husband's whereabouts and schedule, she would call her daughter in order to conspire how to best strike down James.

Despite all the affirmation against her, one person stood by Marcia's side and rallied for her freedom – her own daughter, Shaina. In her heartfelt testimony, she knowingly took the stand and revealed damning evidence that confirmed her guilt in the murder. Unafraid of taking full responsibility for the crimes she committed, Shaina claimed to the jurors that she had executed her father as a way to end the constant fighting in her household – independent of any goading from Marcia. From there, she went on in detail about her stepfather's alleged abuse over the years. Under oath, she claimed that she had been beaten and molested multiple times throughout the years by the man who so badly wanted to be her father. There may have been truth behind her allegations; even the District Attorney assigned to the case conceded that James was the sort of man "who would probably use the belt from time to time" to discipline his children. Whether there was any truth to the story or not, her testimony ultimately did very little to sway the opinion of the court. Prior to taking the stand, Shaina had never made any mention nor allegations of being abused by members of her family, calling to question her overall credibility. In addition, she adamantly proclaimed her mother's complete innocence despite the implications others had made suggesting otherwise. In retrospect, prosecutor Stephanie Stephens reflected, "You've got to give Shaina a little credit, because when her back was against the wall, she did not drop her mother in the grease. But Marcia Kelly, the moment her back was against the wall, she dropped her daughter in the grease." And indeed, Marcia allowed her daughter to take the fall for her.

Ultimately, Marcia Kelly was convicted capital murder despite her daughter's best efforts to deflect the jury's attention from the facts. Although the state of Texas could have opted for the death penalty, it was eventually decided to be too harsh a punishment to pursue. Instead, she was sentenced to life in prison without possibility of parole. After the sentencing she was taken from the courtroom and transported to the Gatesville, Texas Department of Criminal Justice Mountain View Unit. Kelly was not the only one to receive proper punishment from the justice system for the murder of her husband. In separate trials following Marcia's conviction, Colton Weir and Shaina Sepulvado were likewise found guilty of capital murder and sentenced to life in prison without parole. However, as luck would have it, the Supreme Court found in 2012 that the life without parole sentence applied to crimes committed as a juvenile falls under the category of cruel and unusual punishment. In accordance with the US Constitution, the two can apply for re-sentencing and, with some luck, hope for a life outside of captivity. Dallas Christian ended up with a lighter sentence than his companions – after pleading guilty, he received only 40 years behind bars. Additionally, friends of the murderers Billy Loftin and Gary Batchelor were found guilty of lesser charges, including tampering with crucial evidence.

* * *

Since mother and daughter have been locked away, the story has continued to captivate the local community. Some are haunted by the acts the women committed - others believe the sentencing to be a horrible mistake.

Though nearly a decade has passed since the sentencing, Marcia Kelly remains in the Mountain View Unit to this day. She continues to insist upon her innocence, firmly denying having had any involvement in her husband's death. She has appealed several times to have her ruling overturned. Each attempt has been fruitless, and it's likely that Marcia will spend the rest of her life in a cell. Shaina, on the other hand, has made the most of the situation and even maintains relationships with those roaming the outside world. Through a prison pen pal system, she was able to strike up a romantic relationship with fellow Nacogdoches resident J. Patrick Capps. After some correspondence, the two eventually married.

Capps sincere belief in Shaina's testimony led him to create a web campaign in an attempt to free Marcia. The site he created on her behalf included Marcia's detailed version of events leading up to and following the crime. However, the site has since been taken down. Capps was stopped from publically speaking out on the matter when he was convicted of posting falsified documents online, including a phony notarized statement alleging to overturn the final verdict signed by a state deputy. But Capps' stunt represents just the tip of the iceberg of support both women have received over the years. Guilty verdicts aside, many remain sympathetic to the circumstances mother and daughter have faced. In fact, nearly 1500 people have signed an online petition to free Shaina, believing her abuse allegations to be true and her sentencing to be unfair due to her mental capabilities and youth.

As time has passed, the story has attracted attention far beyond the rural suburbs of East Texas. In 2011, TLC's Prison Diaries featured the case - Snapped, a true crime television series airing on Oxygen followed the story shortly afterward. Later on, Investigation Discovery featured Marcia Kelly and her daughter on two separate programs, Redrum and Fatal Vows. Dozens of articles surrounding the case have been published by local and national news sources, catching the eyes of readers across the United States.

In many ways, Marcia Kelly is a relatable character. Plenty of people struggle through unhappy marriages weighed down with baggage. Tens of thousands of people fight each day to continue putting food on their kitchen tables. The description of Cushing, Texas falls in line with many tiny towns scattered throughout the countryside. What truly sticks out about Marcia is the way that she chose to deal with the frustrations that so many of us face on a daily basis. Because of her choice, Nacogdoches county may never feel quite as safe as it once did. Frightening and fascinating, the fact that's most disturbing of all is that Marcia wasn't a cold blooded psychopath. Instead, she was a calculating individual looking for more than her life in Cushing could offer – a woman with dreams that may fall in line with many of our own.

BABY KILLER : THE TRUE STORY OF CHRISTINA MARIE RIGGS

87

DIANE ULLMER

Christina Riggs had all the drugs she needed.

She had filled her prescription for the anti-depressant Elavil at the pharmacy. She had stolen morphine and potassium chloride from the hospital. Now all she had to do was follow through.

"Kids," she bellowed out from the living room table. "Vitamins!"

The two sleepy-eyed children emerged from their bedroom. Christina gave them a small amount of Elavil, dropping the pill in their mouth and watching them drink it down with a cup of water.

A few minutes later, she carried them both back to bed.

Looking down at her two young children, she began to sob.

Shelby, just two years old, in her pink jumper. Justin, five years old, in his white pajamas with battleship designs.

I have to do this. Things will only get worse for them.

THE GREATEST TABOO

Christina Marie Riggs was twenty-six years when she decided to kill her children.

"A mother is supposed to protect her own children," Riggs' Defense Attorney John Wesley Hall Jr. said. "And here she didn't and it doesn't make sense. Two defenseless children that didn't know what was coming."

After Christina sedated her children, she proceeded with her plan of injecting them with potassium chloride. She knew that the drug was administered for lethal injection executions and would stop the heart within minutes.

What she didn't know was that the drug had to be administered in a diluted form. If it is injected without any dilution, it will burn through the skin then burst through the vein.

Ignorant of the consequences, Christina injected the lethal cocktail into her son Justin first.

She wanted a painless death. She did not want her children to go through life suffering like she did.

But then her son woke up screaming.

The potassium chloride she injected was binding and burning through his blood vessel linings.

He cried and cried and wouldn't stop.

Christina began crying herself...

CHILDHOOD TRAUMA

Christina Riggs had a troubled childhood growing up in Oklahoma City, OK.

She was separated from her brothers and sisters after her parent's divorce. Raised alone by her mother, she detailed in a prison diary sexual abuses that took place in her childhood.

She wrote how her stepbrother sexually abusing her from the age of seven to thirteen. At the age of thirteen, she was molested by a neighbor as well.

By the time she entered her teenage years, Christina was obese, using food as an emotional outlet. She also began abusing alcohol and marijuana.

"She indulged in overeating because she didn't want to appear attractive," forensic psychologist Paula Orange said. "That behavior was part of a psychological response to being molested. 'If I become fat and ugly then he won't want me anymore.' No one will bother me, no one will hurt me."

In her teenage years, however, Christina began to use sex as a way to get what she wanted, which was love.

"It isn't uncommon for abused young women to become very promiscuous," Orange said. "It is learned behavior. She became defective, if you will, and should have gotten help. Unfortunately, this is not a good recipe for someone who wants to have a healthy stable relationship and raise children."

"I felt that no boy liked me because of my weight," Christina wrote in her journal. "So I became sexually promiscuous because I thought that was the only way I could have a boyfriend."

She became pregnant by the age of sixteen but gave the baby boy up for adoption.

After high school, Christina went to a vocational school to become a licensed practical nurse (LPN). She obtained employment as a home care nurse and then later worked full-time at a VA hospital.

Her dating life remained steady albeit unsuccessful. She went from one man to the next, dating a Navy ensign named Jon Riggs and a bouncer before meeting Timothy Thompson. Thompson was an Air Force private at Tinker Air Force Base.

Three years after her first child, Christina would become pregnant with Timothy's baby. She informed Timothy her pregnancy the day before he was to be discharged from the Air Force.

Timothy, however, did not take the news well. He would not accept responsibility and moved back to his native Minnesota.

"Chrissy's luck with men was about zero to nothing," Carol Thomas, Christina's mother said.

But while her relationship ended with Timothy, Christina hooked back up with Jon Riggs who returned home after being on leave with the Navy.

"It was great," Christina wrote. "He felt the baby's first kick. As far as he was concerned, it was his baby."

Justin Thomas was born on June 7th, 1992.

"As I held Justin in my arms and looked into his little face, I became so scared," Christina wrote. "Would I be a good Mom? Could I give him all he needed?"

Riggs would move in with Christina and the two hoped for the best. Christina would become pregnant again and the couple would marry in July of 1993.

But misfortune would strike again as Christina would suffer a miscarriage on her wedding night.

The marriage would go south from there as Christina alternated between being depressed to having suicidal thoughts. She blamed her mental state on her birth control medication and a doctor gave her the anti-depressant Prozac.

The medication worked for a while but then Christina inexplicably stopped taking the drug. She kept her sadness to herself and didn't want to burden others with her problems.

"She's always been that way," Christina's mother said. "If I pushed her hard she might get mad and tell me what was going on."

By 1994, Christina would become pregnant and deliver a healthy baby girl in December named Shelby. This would mark the high point of Christina's life as "Sissie" and "Bubbie", the two nicknames for her children, brought immeasurable joy into her life.

She would write that it was the happiest time of her life as both she and Jon cried when they held their new baby in their arms. Things were happy for once in her life.

Christina continued to work as a vocational nurse and was assigned to work at a triage station which served to help the victims of the Oklahoma City Federal Building terrorist bombing. She would suffer post-traumatic stress disorder as a result. Later at her trial, the prosecuting attorneys would argue that the hospital had no record of Christina serving after the bombing. This may be nitpicking as authorities were lenient with record keeping during that urgent situation.

STRESS AND STRAIN

A year later, the couple would move to Sherwood, Arkansas to be closer to Christina's mother, Carole.

Carole worked as a food service worker at Baptist Hospital and Christina was able to find a job there as well, once again working as a licensed practical nurse.

The children go on to have ailments that would stress out the already fragile Christina. Shelby would have chronic ear infections that made doctor visits a routine thing. Justin was diagnosed with attention deficit disorder and his hyper nature would grate on the nerves of his parents.

Financial difficulties and the stress of running a family would put a strain on the marriage and the couple would eventually divorce. Her husband, Jon Riggs, had a volatile temper that he eventually took out on the young Justin. Jon would punch Justin in the abdomen with such force that the young boy had to go to the emergency room.

Jon would then abandon the family.

"Justin would say, 'My Daddy hurt me, and then he went away,' " Christina's mother recalled.

Christina would receive limited child support from Jon and had to work long hours to provide for her family. The more hours she worked, the more she had to pay for daycare which proved to be a daily traumatic event.

Shelby would cry as Christina would leave her at the facility.

"She was beating on the glass, yelling, 'Mama! Mama!' " Christina recalled.

Despite her increased efforts, Christina could not get ahead financially. She began writing bad checks. Bills remained unpaid. Car insurance. Car registration. Lights and utilities.

"I started out in a boat with a small hole," Christina said. "But the hole kept getting bigger, and no matter how hard you bail, you keep sinking. I was tired and I gave up. Suicide seemed like the only thing."

A HISTORY OF MENTAL ILLNESS

Christina had a cousin that killed herself. Her mother had also tried to kill herself when Christina was a baby. Her grandmother was committed to a mental institution.

But Christina would outdo them all in one fateful night.

"Just speaking in general," Orange said. "When mothers kill their children they do not poison them. In the case of Christina, she was applying what she thought would be a lethal injection."

But even with a history of mental illness in the family, nobody could have predicted how the sweet and caring Christina could commit such a heinous crime.

"Chrissy always wanted to help people," Christina's sister, Elizabeth Nottingham said. "She was always helping someone."

But Nottingham had some valuable psychological insight on her sister. She was a mental health counselor and had been close to Christina.

She wanted to know what drove her sister to kill her own children. After her sister's arrest, she began fishing around her house, looking for some kind of clue, a sign that everyone had missed.

"I was almost hoping to find that she wasn't a good parent," Nottingham said. "Then I could be mad at her. You know, I went through her house with a fine toothed comb. All the chemicals were locked away. The food was in the refrigerator. Even pictures of their fathers was in their room above each of their beds. She was great with the kids."

MORE TROUBLE WITH MEN

What Christina's sister would find out was that she simply could not find a decent man. That one relationship where everything would be ideal.

After her divorce from Jon, Christina would enter into another relationship which again would not go well.

"The guy didn't just break her heart," Nottingham said. "But took her credit card. I mean, it's one thing to have someone dump you, it's another to have someone rip you off and leave you destitute too."

After this break-up, Christina would sit at her dining room table both broke and broken-hearted. She had no man in her life. She had no means to pay her family's bills.

Seeing only dark lights ahead, Christina would lapse into a deep depression. She went to her doctor again who prescribed her more Prozac which used irregularly.

"She may have stopped taking the Prozac when she killed the babies," Orange said. "When someone just stops that medication cold-turkey it can have some side effects like increased irritability, irrational mood changes, and an even deeper depression."

"So she had the perfect storm brewing," Nottingham said. "She had depression, she had all of these personal failures. You know, people talk about having rainy days and Mondays. And in fact 'Rainy days and Mondays' was the CD that was in her CD player."

BACK TO THAT FATEFUL NIGHT

Christina had to kill herself. Her emotional bank account had been overdrawn for years.

But she couldn't stand the thought of leaving her children alone.

"If she left the kids behind," Hall Jnr said. "She was afraid that the children would be separated, go to their father's, for instance, and be split up."

"She just thought there was no other way out," Nottingham said. "She thought that no one else would take care of her kids. And that they would be better off, in her mind, she was saving them from future sadness."

With Justin screaming in pain, Christina panicked. She began sobbing but whatever remain of her maternal instinct kicked in and she tried to inject him with morphine.

Toxicology reports didn't reveal whether or not she did this.

But what she did do was suffocate her young son with a pillow. Sobbing, she then did the same deed to her baby daughter, Shelby.

Shaking with adrenaline and grief, Christina wobbled on shaky legs back to her living room. She took out her bottle of Elavil, an anti-depressant, and swallowed the remaining twenty-eight pills. Her nerves calming, she tried injecting the potassium chloride into her own arm.

The chemical burn right through her vein, collapsing it.

The drugs began taking effect and Christina fainted to the floor, hoping her nightmare would finally end.

THE DAY AFTER

The lethal mixture had burned a half-inch hole into Christina's arm. She didn't show up for work the next day and her mother called her cell phone and land line repeatedly.

Worried that she received no response, Carole drove to Christina's apartment and let herself in.

To her horror, she thought everyone was dead, including Christina.

"All I could do was turn around and around and scream and holler, 'No. No. No.' There's no way to describe how I felt."

Frantic, she called 911 and yelling into the phone, "My daughter and babies are dead."

Paramedics would arrive.

The children were dead.

But the medics were able to resuscitate Christina. She was transported to the intensive care unit and was kept under guard by the police.

"I had to do it so I wouldn't leave them behind," Christina was overheard saying in her hospital room. The treating physician, Dr. Jim Rice, would later testify that Christina as "combative at times" and "just incoherent and not really making any sense."

As soon as Christina became reasonably coherent, she was taken to the police station for booking.

THE INTERROGATION

On November 6th, 1997, Christina was interrogated by a Detective Jones and Detective Sharon Williams.

"Christina, what we are doing is investigating the death of your two babies. Do you want to tell us what happened?" Jones asked.

"I killed them," Christina said, crying.

"What did you say?"

"I said-"

"Did you say you killed them?"

"I'm sorry."

"How did you go about doing that?" Jones asked.

"I got some bottles and stuff from here...I need a cigarette...Darvocet."

"Are you saying that you got some medicine from the hospital?"

Christina nodded.

"Christina, how did you do it? Did you give them an injection? Did you give them a shot?"

"I tried to ... and ... I did it with Justin because I figured with him being the oldest one that he would give me more problems. So, I tried it with him and I thought it would just stop his heart. But it hurt. Oh, he said it hurt ...It didn't work, he just kept calling, 'Momma! Momma! Momma!' I just figured it was too late now because I had no place to turn back to. I cleaned out my checking account and gave my mother all the money I had."

"Christina, why did you do this?" Jones asked.

"Because I wanted to die," Christina said, crying again. "But I didn't want to die and leave my kids behind or for them to be a burden to somebody else. I didn't want them to think I didn't love them and I didn't want them to grow up separately because they have two different Daddies. And I knew if I passed away they would be fighting my Mother for custody and I didn't want that for nobody."

"You felt like you were doing it for the kids' sake?"

"In a way, yeah... my piece of mind."

"Christina, did you really want to die?"

Christina didn't respond. She continued crying.

"And you felt it would be better if your children just die with you and ... were the children already dead before you took your medicine?"

"Yes."

"How long had they been dead before you took your medicine?"

"About twenty minutes."

"About twenty minutes?"

"That's because I drank and got up and smoked a cigarette and got back and sit for a minute and...I was like, 'Okay, I'm going to do it now. I can't turn back now because you've already killed Justin.' And ... so I did it."

"What time did you give them the medicine? Do you remember?"

"Justin about 10:15 or 10:30."

"10:15 or 10:30 in the morning?"

"No, in the evening."

"Oh, in the evening?"

"Last night."

"Okay."

"Then I smoked another cigarette and waited," Christina paused. "And suffocated Shelby."

"You suffocated Shelby? What did ... how did you suffocate her?"

"I put a pillow over her head."

"Okay, Did you ... Had you given her any medicine at all, or ... any of the Morphine or the Potassium Chloride?"

"I slipped them ... I made them drink half of an Elavil because I figured that would make them sleep a little bit better so that it wouldn't wake them."

"So, Shelby, you killed her with a pillow. You suffocated her. And what about the little boy. How did you do him?"

"I gave him the medicine and when it didn't work."

"You suffocated him too?"

"Yes."

"With a pillow? Were they fighting while you suffocated them?"

"Justin did. Shelby a little bit but not much," Christina began to cry again.

"When did you decide to do this, Christina? On what day did you decide to do this?"

"Uh ... the best I remember it was Sunday night or Saturday night because we was out talking and this and that and the other ... and they caught me."

"Who caught you?"

"I was depressed. I was thinking about what was going on in my life and that things aren't always working for me and..."

"When did you get those drugs from the hospital?"

"When? Yesterday."

"Yesterday? You mean the day that you killed them? Is that the day that you got the drugs? The last was it ... "

"Was it the last day that you worked at the hospital or the day before that? "I think ...""

"When you got ... "

"I got the drugs and I gave them to my kids. That's the only drugs that I had in my hand. And I know that there was three Valiums in a vial in there, but there wasn't enough to even cover the jar up and put it in my pocket and bring them home. And I know I should have thought better ... had somebody rinsing with me, but ... they were just what came home in my pockets."

"Did you know what you were going to do when you took the drugs from the hospital? Did you have intentions of giving them to your children? And how many days did you think about this before you killed your children?"

"About three weeks. Two weeks."

"Two or three weeks. In other words, you've been thinking about doing this for the last two or three weeks? What made you decide to just go ahead and do it?"

"I just can't take it no more."

"You couldn't take it anymore."

"I felt like I was out of control," Christina said.

"Did you just feel like your life was in a mess? Had you talked to anybody about this? Your Mom or anybody?"

"I've tried to talk to people about what I feel and what I think and they were just like, 'I don't have time right now. We'll do it some other time.' So, I just got to where I don't care anymore. I tried but they can't give me no help."

"So you just felt like nobody was listening to you? Okay, Christina ...Christina, do you have anything more to say about your babies or anything? "I wish I hadn't done it now."

Christina would then go on an incoherent ramble, explaining how she saw her mother riding down an escalator with a bunch of old people. The detectives, however, got the damning evidence they needed and ended the interrogation.

PRISON AND JAIL

Christina would find a hostile environment in prison. The majority of her fellow prisoners were women who were taken away from their children by force. They had contempt for Christina's crime.

One inmate spat in her face and her life was threatened.

Christina was then moved to an isolated cell where she remained until her trial.

She would be charged with two counts of first-degree murder which was punishable by death in the state of Arkansas.

"We tried to show that she was under extreme emotional disturbance," Hall Jr said. "To justify either not imposing the death penalty or hopefully finding her guilty of second-degree murder."

"I just hope that out of all her misery," Nottingham said. "The sadness of our family. That we can shed some light on the causes of this for other people and that maybe they'll be able to look at the symptoms and look at the situations and maybe intervene for someone else."

But the prosecuting attorney, as well as the community, believed that Christina was guilty of performing a selfish act, an act wherein she tried to free herself from motherhood.

The most damning evidence at the trial, aside from the interrogation tapes, would be the account of the physicians.

One doctor would testify that it would take three to six minutes to suffocate someone to death. Because of that time period, the jurors would be able to envision how Christina commit a willful act of murder. Christina had, in essence, a struggling toddler under her pillow for about three to six minutes...suffocating to death.

"They just wanted her to be evil," Nottingham said of the prosecuting attorney's intent. "It was easier that way."

"Essentially, what the jury saw was that she was self-centered," argued Pulaski Prosecuting Attorney Larry Jegley. "That she viewed the children as an inconvenience and an interference with what she wanted to pursue. She placed her interests above those of the children."

Jegley argued that Christina was a self-centered and premeditated murderer. He brought up the fact that she had locked the children up in the house (according to a neighbor) in order that she could go out to a Karaoke party. He urged the jury not to buy into her manipulation to feel sorry for her. "There were lots of people who have it worse than she did."

The jury would side with the prosecution and find Christina guilty after a very short deliberation period.

THE IRONY

Christina Riggs would be sentenced to death by lethal injection via potassium chloride...The same method that she used to try to kill her children and herself.

"It was a cruel irony that they finished what she started," Hall Jr said. "Almost the exact same way except she was strapped down to a table."

Christina would appeal the sentencing but did so with reluctance. She wanted to die.

"I'll be with my children and with God," Christina said. "I'll be where there's no more pain. Maybe I'll find some peace."

Her defense attorney John Wesley Hall Jr was allowed to witness the execution.

"You can see their face," Hall Jr said. "It allows them to say their last words. The face changes color as the drugs take effect. You turn gray. The skin turns gray. And it's rather shocking to watch it happen."

"She was so depressed that it became this black sheet over her eyes that she couldn't see through," Orange said. "She wanted to spare her own children from the kind of life that she had. She had lost complete hope and really over thought things. That's how her depression warped her. It warped her enough to think that she was doing her children a favor by killing them."

Christina was sent to death row and was haunted by the memories of her children. She openly stated that she tried "not to think about them" because when she did it was like someone "ripping them away from her all over again."

"A lot of regret," Christina said. "That's what goes through my mind, day-in, day-out. God's punishing me. He let me live so I would suffer."

Riggs was flown in from McPherson Jail to Cummins in order to prep for her execution. She would be administered the lethal injection at 9:28 PM CDT on May 2nd, 2000.

"No words can express just how sorry I am for taking the lives of my babies," Riggs said in a prepared statement. "No way I can make up for or take away the pain I have caused everyone who knew and loved them. I love you, my babies."

CHRISTA PIKE

Christa Gail Pike, born 10 March 1976, currently sits on Tennessee's death row for the murder of Colleen Slemmer, 19, on 12 January 1995. The murder occurred when Pike was 18 years old. Pike and her then-boyfriend Tadaryl Shipp who was 17 at the time of the murder were convicted of Slemmer's murder and conspiracy to commit murder. Another friend of the defendants and the victim, Shadolla Peterson, also 18 at the time, was convicted as an accessory after the fact and given six years' probation after turning informant. Pike was sentenced to death by electrocution in 1996 and, at the time, she had the distinction of being the youngest woman ever to be sentenced to death, in any state and only the second women given the death penalty in Tennessee.

Early Life

Pike's life reads like a primer for depraved murderers. As a small child, Pike did not enjoy a healthy and supportive bond with her mother, Carissa Hansen, a licensed nurse, allegedly because of her premature birth. Whereas thousands of children are born prematurely and do not resort to criminal behavior Pike's birth was presented as evidence of one possible origin of her poor and troubled behavior. Pike's maternal grandmother was verbally abusive and Pike was raised by her alcoholic and abusive paternal grandmother until the latter's death in 1988 when Pike was 12; after which Pike attempted suicide by overdosing. She was then shuttled back and forth between her divorced parents' homes. In 1989, Pike was kicked out of her father's house for the second and final time due to her unruliness and the alleged sexual abuse of her father's then-two-year old daughter with his second wife.

Prior to the murder, experts assert that there were myriad indications that Pike was seriously disturbed; however, nobody who may have suspected this sought help for the increasingly disobedient and incorrigible young lady. According to Pike's mother, she was problematic since the age of eight and the two of them had a contentious relationship due to Pike's fluctuating and troubling behavior. Her mother asserted that by age nine Pike was growing marijuana in pots at their home and had been permitted to have a live-in boyfriend at age 14. At one point—in an effort to improve their relationship—Hansen suggested that she and Pike smoke marijuana together. Hansen mistakenly believed that cultivating a friendship with her daughter would cultivate the necessary bond Pike had been lacking her entire life. At one point, one of her mother's boyfriends whipped Pike with a belt which prompted her to wield a butcher knife against him before he was subsequently arrested. Hansen also admitted that Pike had repeatedly lied to and stolen from her. In several interviews with Hansen throughout Pike's trial and seemingly endless appeals, she admitted repeatedly that she was a terrible mother and should have spent more time with her daughter.

Pike's aunt, Carrie Ross, provided insight into Pike's upbringing when she testified that she disallowed her own children from associating with Pike because she lived in a filthy house that had zero ground rules and that Pike was a pathological liar of whom she was somewhat afraid. She also admitted that there was a history of substance abuse in Pike's family. Ross also stated that on the few occasions that Pike actually visited her she behaved like a little girl and engaged in Barbie and dress-up play with her eleven-year-old cousin. Further, there were some allegations that Pike may have been sexually abused but these were neither confirmed nor denied.

Pike's father, Glenn Pike testified that he did, in fact, kick his daughter out of his house multiple times; the last time being in 1989 after the aforementioned allegations that Pike sexually abused her two-year old half-sister. He admitted that he had signed adoption papers for Pike prior to her 18th birthday and that during the times she resided with him she was manipulative, disobedient, and dishonest.

After dropping out of high school, Pike began Job Corps classes in computer programming. Job Corps is a government-based organization that provides occupational and vocational training to underprivileged and troubled teens. It was at the now-defunct Job Corps center in Knoxville where she met Shipp, Slemmer, and Peterson. While Job Corps seeks to promote prosocial behavior and foster a strong desire among its participants to learn a vocation and secure a more promising future than might have been previously the case, this program is also known to cultivate criminal activity, likely due to the association among its participants; many of whom already had problematic behavior.

Evidence of Premeditation

On 11 January 1995, the day before the actual homicide, Pike told friend and co-Job Corps student Kim Iloilo that she was planning to kill Slemmer because she "just felt mean that day." Iloilo discounted Pike's statement as nothing more than merely talk; however, the following evening at approximately 8:00 p.m. Iloilo witnessed Pike, Shipp, Peterson, and Slemmer leaving the Job Corps center. When Iloilo saw Pike, Shipp, and Peterson returning at approximately 10:15 p.m. without Slemmer she, again, thought nothing of it. Even when Pike visited Iloilo's dorm room at 11:00 p.m. that night and confessed to killing Slemmer—as well as showing Iloilo what Pike identified as a piece of Slemmer's skull—Iloilo still failed to tell anyone. Later, at Pike's trial, Iloilo testified that while Pike was iterating the events of the murder she was oddly smiling, singing, and dancing around the room. The following morning Iloilo asked Pike what she was going to do with the piece of skull. Pike nonchalantly replied that she had it in her pocket and was, in fact, eating breakfast with it.

Pike also told another student, Stephanie Wilson, a similar account the following day and proudly described the brown spots on her shoes as blood. Not unlike Iloilo, Wilson failed to immediately report anything.

The Crime Scene

On 13 January, officers from the University of Tennessee and Knoxville Police Departments were dispatched to greenhouses on the University's agricultural campus in Tyson Park where a University grounds department employee reported finding, at approximately 8:05 a.m., what he assumed to be a dead animal. The gruesome discovery was a corpse that turned out to be Colleen Slemmer. She was naked from the waist up; her throat was cut; her head had been bludgeoned; and she had various cuts all over her arms, throat, and torso—including a pentagram that had been carved into her chest. Officer John Terry Johnson who testified at Pike's trial described Slemmer's body as so badly beaten that she was unrecognizable as a human being. He also stated that he thought he was looking at her face when, in reality,

Slemmer was lying face-down in the dirt and debris where Pike, Shipp, and Peterson had left her.

There was additional evidence and testimony that the crime scene encompassed an area that measured 100 feet long by 60 feet wide; an astounding 6,000 square feet in area. Despite the area being muddy and wet there was ample evidence of a physical struggle with trampled bushes, a considerable amount of blood, body drag marks, and hand and knee prints. Thirty feet from Slemmer's body was a large pool of blood which suggested that Slemmer was attacked in one area and then dragged to where her body was later found. Slemmer's shirt and bra were also discovered at the crime scene, as well as a bloody rag that Pike admitted to tying over Slemmer's mouth at one point to keep her from screaming.

Disturbingly, University of Tennessee police officer Harold James Underwood, Jr., who was the officer assigned to secure the crime scene, testified at trial that Pike and a few other females came to the scene between four and five p.m. the day of the discovery and before Pike was even considered to be a suspect. Underwood stated that Pike had asked why the wooded area was marked off, who the victim was, and whether police had any leads as to who the suspect or suspects were. He particularly recalled Pike's odd behavior—moving around a lot while giggling amusedly—and that she wore a necklace in the shape of a pentagram. The following day, during briefing when informed that the victim had a pentagram carved into her chest, Underwood reported Pike's behavior and necklace to his supervisors.

Autopsy and Findings

During Slemmer's autopsy, the medical examiner, Dr. Sandra Elkins, had to identify the victim's body from dental records because her head was so bludgeoned that she was unrecognizable. After cleaning up Slemmer's body which was clad only in jeans, socks, and shoes, and covered with dirt and twigs, Dr. Elkins began cataloging Slemmer's wounds. Due to the sheer number of wounds on her back, arms, abdomen, and chest, and the fact that following department policy which stated that each individual wound be assigned a letter of the alphabet, when Dr. Elkins reached double letters she, instead, individually catalogued only the most serious wounds and that there were innumerable other superficial and defensive wounds. Among the most serious cuts was a six-inch gaping wound across Slemmer's throat that was deep enough to penetrate the fat and muscles in her neck as well as the aforementioned pentagram. Additional injuries included fresh bruising which Dr. Elkins asserted was consistent with crawling.

Cause of death was ultimately attributed to blunt force trauma to the head. Dr. Elkins surmised that Slemmer's head was hit with the asphalt at least four times—two to the left side, one over the right eye, and one to the nose—which collectively resulted in multiple and extensive skull fractures. One of these blows was to the left side of Slemmer's head—which, according to Dr. Elkins, occurred with the right side of the victim's head against a firm surface. This blow only fractured her skull but also imbedded a portion of Slemmer's skull into her head and contained black particles from the piece of asphalt determined to be the murder weapon.

Even more tragic was Dr. Elkins' findings that none of Slemmer's other wounds would have rendered her unconscious and evidence of active blood flow around the wounds and blood in her sinus cavity indicated that Slemmer was alive during the severe torture she suffered before being killed.

Arrest and Confession

The police quickly connected Pike to the homicide thanks to the piece of Slemmer's skull discovered in Pike's jacket pocket. Pike had left this jacket hanging on the back of a chair in Job Corps Orientation Specialist Robert A. Pollock's office on 13 January after meeting with him about a misplaced ID card. Pike's jacket remained in Pollock's office from 4:00 p.m. on 13 January until 7:30 a.m. on 17 January. After learning over the weekend that Pike was a suspect in Slemmer's murder investigation, Pollock immediately gave the jacket to William Hudson, the Job Corps' safety and security captain who turned it over to Knoxville Police Department Officer Arthur Bohanan. At trial, Bohanan would testify that he found a small piece of bone in one of the pockets and presented it to Dr. Murray Marks, a University of Tennessee forensic anthropologist who was reconstructing Slemmer's decapitated skull and the piece in Pike's jacket pocket fit perfectly into an area where a portion of her skull was missing at the time of the victim's discovery.

When confronted with this evidence and subsequently arrested, Pike waived her *Miranda* protections and confessed to the murder and permitted officers to search her dorm room where the blood-soaked jeans she wore the previous night were found. Additionally, Pike led officers to a trash can at a nearby Texaco station on Cumberland Avenue where she had disposed of Slemmer's ID and a pair of gloves Pike had been wearing at the time of the homicide.

Pike's transcribed confession was 46 pages long.

In it, Pike admitted that there was animosity between Slemmer and her because Pike was convinced that Slemmer was a rival for the affections of her boyfriend, Shipp, and that Slemmer was trying to get Pike kicked out of the Job Corps program so she could have Shipp for herself. Pike also claimed that she had awakened one night to find Slemmer standing above her with a box cutter; however, there is no evidence of this allegation. Instead, Slemmer had repeatedly called her mother, May Martinez, to tell her she was afraid of Pike who she had awakened to find in her room and that she wanted to come home; to which Slemmer's mother said that she couldn't because she had signed a contract. Pike stated that she had only planned to fight Slemmer to stop her from running her mouth. On that fateful night of 12 January, Pike, Slemmer, Shipp, and Peterson signed the Job Corps logbook as they were leaving for an outing Slemmer believed was to smoke marijuana en route to a video store so that Pike and she could try to work out their problems.

When the group entered a tunnel at the edge of Tyson Park, Slemmer likely felt that something was not quite right and proceeded to ask Pike where they were going and whether there was, in fact, any marijuana. These questions irritated Pike who began the brutal assault shortly thereafter after they had gone deeply enough into the woods so that nobody could hear them that led to Slemmer's murder.

Pike confessed to initially slamming Slemmer's head into her knee and then throwing her to the ground where Pike continually punched, kicked, and slammed Slemmer's head into the concrete, screaming, "the bi*ch won't die" and that she wanted "to see [Slemmer's] brains flow." According to witnesses Shipp and Peterson, as Slemmer continued to plead with Pike to stop, Pike got angrier and more brutal. Slemmer offered to return to her Florida home, leave her belongings at the Job Corps center, and not tell anyone what happened; however, Pike became more enraged and yelled at Slemmer to be quiet because "it was harder to hurt someone who was talking to you."

In addition to the savage beating, Slemmer had been cut innumerable times with a box cutter and a mini meat cleaver (that Pike had allegedly borrowed from another Job Corps student) to her torso, arms, face, and back including having had her throat slit six times prior to the fatal blow that resulted from having her head crushed by a piece of asphalt. There was also a pentagram carved into Slemmer's chest; however, Pike asserted that Shipp had done that. Pike also confessed to "just watching Slemmer bleed" when the victim got up and tried to run away. Pike admitted to cutting Slemmer's back: "the big long cut."

After the murder, Pike stated that she and Shipp washed their hands and shoes in a nearby mud puddle to conceal the blood, dumped the box cutter, and Pike returned the meat cleaver to the person from which she borrowed it. This person has never been identified.

The physical evidence and co-defendant testimony suggested that the assault and murder lasted from 30 minutes to an hour and consisted of Slemmer repeatedly trying to get up and run away but was prevented from doing so by the co-defendants who also, as Pike testified, contributed to the physical assault by throwing rocks at Slemmer's head and holding her down so she couldn't run away. Later, Pike would testify that she heard voices in her head overriding Slemmer's continual screaming, telling her that she needed to prevent Slemmer from filing charges against her for attempted murder. Pike also admitted that at one point she thought she had heard a noise and went to investigate it to ensure that they were alone, as well as alleging that during the assault she heard Slemmer breathing in blood and jerking but did not let this assuage her anger as Pike continued her savagery.

Even more troublesome, a police video recorded after Pike's confession shows Pike smiling and providing extensive details about the crime at the crime scene, oftentimes mimicking her actions that evening. Many have said that her demeanor on the recording was eerily similar to that of a little girl who was excited and happy that she had experienced the best day of her life and had no problem talking about the events that transpired, the heinousness of her actions, and how she felt about it all.

The facts of the homicide are not nor have they ever been in dispute, thanks to an abundance of evidence. Pike's confession, and witness testimony at the trial.

Pre-Trial Examination

Prior to her trial, Pike was given a battery of assessment tests and examined by numerous psychiatrists including clinical psychologist Dr. Eric Engum who found her to be extremely bright as evidenced by an I.Q. of 111—in the 77th percentile of the general population—which he believed to be remarkable given her difficult childhood and lack of formal schooling beyond the ninth grade. Dr. Engum also found that

Pike had excellent reasoning, problem solving, language, and analytic skills, and was also quite adept at paying attention, sustaining concentration, and sequencing information. Dr. Engum concluded that Pike was legally sane and had no brain damage which has frequently been demonstrated to cause violent behavior in some individuals.

Of particular interest was that Pike was found to be marijuana- and inhalant-dependent and also diagnosed with borderline personality disorder. Whereas there are some similarities between borderline personality disorder and antisocial personality disorder such as impulsivity, irritability, aggression, and a self-image that fluctuates between self-aggrandizement and despair, there are several differences. Individuals with borderline personality disorder differ from those with antisocial behavior in that the former—which primarily affects females—is characterized by a lack of remorse, self-destructiveness, black-and-white thinking, alcohol and/or drug use or abuse, unstable relationships characterized by fear of abandonment and extreme swings between love and hate, difficulty in achieving academic and vocational goals, and are more likely to have been sexually abused; while the latter—which affects disproportionately more males—is characterized by a lack of affect and remorse, emptiness, and an ultimate goal of self-preservation.

Pike demonstrated all of the aforementioned characteristics of borderline personality disorder which makes it easier—but not justifiably so—to comprehend how her intense jealousy of Slemmer and fear of losing Shipp made her commit her atrocious acts. In addition to her fear of abandonment, Pike also abused drugs, was likely sexually abused, had contentious relationships, and displayed zero remorse. Dr. Engum surmised that Pike did not act with premeditation or deliberation in Slemmer's murder but, instead, in a manner that was consistent with borderline personality disorder. More simply, Pike had lost control. However, on cross-examination Dr. Engum admitted that Pike's deliberate luring of Slemmer, that she carved a pentagram in the victim's chest, that she brought weapons with her, and that she bashed Slemmer's head into the concrete does, in fact, constitute deliberateness.

That Pike was overjoyed and singing in Iloilo's room describing the murder while dancing around with the portion of Slemmer's skull Pike had taken as a trophy further supported Dr. Engum's diagnosis of borderline personality disorder because she had eliminated who she perceived was in competition for her boyfriend, Shipp, and, therefore, could continue her relationship with him. When questioned about the piece of skull Pike had taken, Dr. Engum said that Pike had no identity and her actions of taking and displaying the skull was a way to get recognition, no matter how misleading and distorted said recognition might be. In fact, after her conviction and sentencing Pike wrote a letter to Shipp which was intercepted by jail personnel that stated that even though she tried to be "nice" to Slemmer by bashing in her head instead of letting her bleed to death she was still sentenced to "fry."

The Trial

There was an abundance of evidence presented at the trial. Physical evidence consisted of crime scene photographs, autopsy reports, bloody clothing, and the piece of Slemmer's skull Pike had taken as a trophy. With respect to this skull piece, Dr. Elkins presented Slemmer's decapitated skull that was reconstructed by Dr. Marks to explain the victim's injuries. The skull presented at trial was complete except for a portion that was missing on the left side of Slemmer's skull. Dr. Elkins demonstrated that the piece of skull found in Pike's jacket fit perfectly into this spot, much to the chagrin of Slemmer's mother who, in a taped interview, stated that Pike was oftentimes giggling and passing notes to her mother and defense attorney during the trial, not unlike an immature middle-schooler.

At the trial, the State introduced photographs taken of Pike and Shipp at the Knoxville Police Department in which both were wearing pentagram necklaces similar to the shape carved into Slemmer's chest. It was presented that both Pike and Shipp dabbled in devil worshiping and other forms of the occult and that Slemmer was a sacrifice for the next day, Friday the 13th. Despite the presence of some type of satanic elements in Slemmer's murder, Dr. William Bernet, Vanderbilt University's psychiatric hospital medical director, testified that the evidence was that of "an adolescent dabbling in Satanism." He further concluded that the concept of collective aggression—or mob mentality—in which a group of people become stimulated and subsequently engage in some type of violent behavior was most assuredly at play in the events leading to Slemmer's death. However, Dr. Bernet ultimately stated that he did not have enough evidence to definitively surmise whether Pike had acted with premeditation or intent when she lured and murdered Slemmer.

Pike was ultimately convicted of first-degree murder and conspiracy to commit first-degree murder after a mere two-and-a-half hours of jury deliberation. The fact that the jury returned guilty verdicts for first-degree murder—and did it so quickly—demonstrate that jurors were convinced that Pike had the requisite mens rea, or mental capacity, to warrant a first-degree murder charge: premeditation and deliberation. Amidst the overwhelming evidence and utter lack of remorse for her actions Pike was sentenced to death by electrocution (Tennessee has since adopted lethal injection for executions but has the prerogative to utilize electrocution if the lethal injection drugs cannot be obtained). Shipp was sentenced to life without parole because his age at the time of the murder was too young to warrant capital punishment and Peterson turned informant and was given six years' probation for her testimony.

Pike's conviction was upheld by the Court of Criminal Appeals and the United States Supreme Court denied certiorari.

Post-Conviction

While incarcerated, Pike demonstrated more evidence of her depravity. In 2001 she tried to murder fellow inmate Patricia Jones by strangling her with a shoelace. Pike alleges that Jones repeatedly tortured her by calling her "fried chicken" and making various demeaning sounds as an affront to what Jones said was the sound that Pike would make when she was electrocuted. The final straw was when Jones physically threatened Pike's friend, fellow devil worshiper Natasha Cornet. Pike said that she jumped atop Jones and choked her with a shoelace so that the much larger and heavier Jones would get off of Cornet. By the time prison guards reached them, Jones was unconscious.

Pike was subsequently convicted of attempted murder despite her prior death sentence because any offense committed while an individual is incarcerated must be adjudicated. During this time, neurology specialist Dr. Jonathan Henry Pincus began investigating Pike's brain to glean some type of knowledge as to why Pike behaved and continued to act violently the way she did when she assaulted Jones. He asserted that every killer he has ever examined share three commonalities: brain damage, a history of abuse, and mental illness. Dr. Pincus alleged that Pike did, in fact, possess all three features and demonstrates all of the requisite features common to serial killers. There is much consensus among professionals that Pike would likely have been a serial killer had she not been caught the first time.

He also testified at Pike's attempted murder trial that her brain's frontal lobes are not "put together properly"; largely due, he claimed, to the fact that Pike's mother drank while she was pregnant with Pike despite denial of this by Pike's mother. It was also brought up that as a child Pike played at the slaughterhouse where her grandfather worked and that she was frequently subjected to pornography and horror movies on the home television screen. He asserted that all of these factors provide insight into how an 18-year old girl could act with such depravity as was the case when Pike murdered Slemmer.

However, the original trial judge, Mary Beth Leibowitz, stated that Pincus' "findings" of brain damage was curious as the defense expert at Pike's original trial who was trying to spare her the death penalty failed to find such evidence.

Forensic psychiatrist William Kenner testified that Pike had suffered from undiagnosed bipolar disorder, the symptoms of which were evident from the time Pike was a "sleepless, talkative adolescent" and likened her to an automobile with cruise control set at 120 miles per hour. Pike's post-conviction defense team alleged that this non-diagnosis justified her requesting a new trial.

In 2002 Pike sought to have her appeal legally stopped and to proceed with her execution. In June of that year Judge Leibowitz granted Pike's request and scheduled an execution date of 19 August 2002. However, a few days later Pike changed her mind and the Tennessee Court of Appeals subsequently stayed her execution. In October 2005, Pike's death sentence was affirmed; however, no execution date has been set at this time.

Pike was again in court in 2007 when her defense team headed by Donald E. Dawson asserted sought a new trial, alleging ineffective assistance of counsel in that her trial defense team failed to introduce evidence supporting Pike's alleged bipolar disorder. During this hearing, Shipp admitted to misinforming investigators and that he, in fact, was primarily responsible for Slemmer's murder. He stated that he was drunk and tired and just wanted the police to leave him alone when he put the onus of blame on Pike. Additional testimony from prior Job Corps student and the defendants' mutual friend Tyrone Comfort stated that Shipp controlled and abused Pike despite her assertions that he was the first male to protect her and she admired the respect and fear he elicited from others. Pike, however, was heavily medicated during this hearing for her alleged bipolar condition and the hearing was rescheduled for April 2008.

During her 2008 hearing, prosecutors portrayed Pike as a cold-blooded vicious killer who not only planned Slemmer's murder but prolonged it for sport, essentially playing cat-and-mouse with Slemmer by allowing her to get up and try to escape and then pushing her back on the ground for additional torture. Ultimately, her request for a new trial was denied.

Pike became newsworthy again in 2012 when she formulated an escape plan with the help of 34-year-old New Jersey resident Donald Kohut who frequently visited Pike in prison but the extent of their relationship remains unknown, and 23-year-old former prison guard Justin Heflin. In a joint investigation by the Tennessee Department of Corrections, the Tennessee Bureau of Investigation, and the New Jersey State Police after receiving information about the plan, both men were arrested and charged with bribery and conspiracy to commit escape, with Heflin charged with an additional facilitation to commit escape charge due to his job as a prison guard. Authorities discovered contraband evidence in the facility which could have only been brought in by a staff member and that Heflin was likely involved. Further investigation demonstrated that Heflin knew Kohut and that Heflin was receiving gifts and money for his assistance in the escape plan. Pike was also charged.

Even more recently, during yet another post-conviction relief hearing in 2015, testimony revealed that Pike was allegedly pregnant at the time of the murder. While this may be true it neither excuses her actions nor provides any potential evidence of legal insanity to justify an affirmative defense of not guilty by reason of mental disease or defect or guilty but mentally ill. Also during this hearing, Slemmer's mother requested the missing piece of her daughter's skull so she could bury the whole of her daughter but was denied as the skull piece remains a critical piece of evidence in Pike's ongoing legal appeals.

Since exhausting the state appeal process, Pike's new defense attorney, Assistant Federal Defender Stephen A. Ferrell, filed a

123-page petition on her behalf alleging that he constitutional rights were violated in both the original 1996 trial and penalty phase and that Tennessee's appellate courts ignored said violations. Among these claims is that capital punishment would amount to cruel and unusual punishment in violation of the Eighth Amendment of the United States Constitution because of Pike's youth, immaturity and mental illness. While Shipp—only 17 at the time of the murder—was too young to warrant imposition of a death sentence, Pike was not. Ferrell alleged that her trial lawyers were incompetent and failed to introduce evidence of mental illness, brain injury, and post-traumatic stress disorder. In response, the state Attorney General submitted a 90-page rebuttal repeatedly asserting that the state courts' ruling were all legally correct. As of the beginning of 2016, this battle continues.

Numerous video interviews of Pike over the past several years show her admitting that she was fully cognizant of her actions and that they were wrong. She stated that she felt as though she was taking out years of abuse on Slemmer and that she committed a horrible atrocity and deserves to be punished; however, she asserts that she deserves life without the possibility of parole for her actions; not the death penalty for the actions of three individuals. She has repeatedly stated that she wishes it was she who died and not Slemmer but such protestations are moot after the fact. One cannot help but wonder if Pike actually means what she says or is simply saying what she thinks others want to her. Knoxville Police Department detective Randy York who worked the case has said that in his lengthy career he has not encountered many people who he believes are evil but that Pike is, indeed, the personification of evil and that she should never be permitted to be around other human beings ever again.

Experts assert that the death penalty is not an effective general deterrent and debate over the morality and legality of capital punishment remains contentious and in the forefront of public discourse and debate. Currently, Tennessee is only one of 38 states which have the death penalty. Whereas women comprise 13% of those arrested for murder, only 2% are sentenced to death and, of those, only 3% are actually executed; primarily due to judges not wanting to sentence women to death. In Tennessee, only two individuals on death row have been executed—both males. The last time a woman was executed in the state was in 1837. Many currently believe that Pike will likely never be executed.

SARA ALDRETE

BILL KEEGAN

EARLY LIFE

Sara Aldrete was born on September 6, 1964 in Matamoros, Tamaulipas, Mexico. As a teen, Sara was allowed to cross the border and attend Porter High School in Brownsville, Texas while her father supported the family working as an electrician. Teachers were fond of Sara as she was a well-behaved student who excelled academically. Her guidance counselor advised her to attend college immediately after graduation but Sara opted to marry instead. At the age of nineteen, she tied the knot with thirty-year old Miguel Zacharias on Halloween Day in 1983. The union did not last last, however, as they were separated and divorced within five months.

Two years later, Sara gained legal status as an American citizen. She enrolled at Texas Southmost College, a two-year school in Brownsville. She had been admitted on a work study program that minimized some of the tuition costs as she worked as both an aerobics teacher and assistant secretary in the school's athletic department.

Sara started classes in January of 1986 as a physical education major. At 6-feet-1 and with model good looks, she was a striking figure around campus.She became one of thirty-three students selected from over a 6,500 member student body to be included in the school's Who's Who directory for 1988. An active student on the campus, she organized a Booster club for the school's soccer squad as well as playing for the girl's volleyball team.

After the dissolution of her marriage, however, she had to move back home with her parents in Matamoros. They had constructed a patio/stairwell outside her second floor room so she could have some semblance of privacy. Sara came home on weekends and during the school breaks, hoping to transfer to a four-year program wherein she could receive a teaching certificate.

Her height and lithe physique caught the eye of many men, in particular Gilberto Sosa, a drug dealer who had ties with the powerful Hernandez family. She began dating Sosa while nurturing an interest in the religion of *Santería*. She learned about the religion's rituals and history during an anthropology class, immediately becoming obsessed. Ironically, this interest would coincide with meeting the man who would take her on a trip into darkness that she would never escape from.

"She would cross that border to Mexico," Lt George Gavito said. "And she would become somebody else."

GODFATHER AND GODMOTHER

Sara was driving through Matamoros on July 30th, 1987 when she nearly got into a car accident with a young man driving a luxury Mercedes-Benz. The young man got out of the car acting apolegetic. Sara was immediately taken by his good looks and well-spoken nature. His introduced himself as Adolfo Constanzo. They exchanged information and Adolfo expressed excitement when he learned that Sara shared the same birthday as his mother.

What Sara didn't know was that the near miss on the Matamoros street was carefully choreographed. Adolfo had been stalking Sara's boyfriend, Gilberto, assessing how much power he had in the drug dealing Hernandez organization.

Adolfo quickly befriended Sara and seduced her with his knowledge of the occult. In a subsequent meeting, Adolfo met the couple together, completely ignoring Gilberto's offer of a handshake and focusing his attention exclusively on Sara.

Later, an anonymous phone call informed Gilberto that Sara was dating someone else. The drug dealer went into a jealous rage and confronted Sara. She denied the allegations but he broke off the relationship anyway.

Sara then turned to Adolfo for comfort. He told her that he knew that Gilberto would break up with her as he had seen her future in a tarot card reading. Adolfo proceeded to "comfort" Sara by seducing her but their physical relationship would not last.

"Sara started dating Constanzo until she found out he was gay," Gavito said. "She said 'no problem'. But he told her what was he was involved in and she introduced him to the Hernandezes. So it was Sara that was the one that connected all of this people together."

Adolfo wanted a meeting with the leader of the Hernandez family, Elio, and Sara arranged for that to happen. Adolfo saw that he could influence drug dealers with his dark magic and earn a nice living for himself. Charming Elio Hernandez would be step one toward that goal.

When Sara returned to the college, her classmates noted that her demeanor changed significantly. Sara obsessed on witchcraft and magic in every conversation. She wanted to argue on the merits between good and evil.

Sara eventually left her studies behind and Adolfo welcomed her into his growing cult. He christened her as "La Madrina", the Godmother. He himself was "El Padrino", the Godfather.

WHO WAS ADOLFO CONSTANZO?

Adolfo was born in Miami, FL on November 1st, 1962 by a fifteen year old girl who would subsequently have three children by three different men. His mother, named Delia Aurora Gonzalez, had her son blessed by a Haitian priest who practiced *palo mayombe*, a form of witchcraft that owes its origins to the Congo but was passed down to Cuba and Puerto Rico with the settlement of slaves.

The boy's mother was excited when the Haitian priest pronounced that her six month old child was "chosen" and "destined for great power."

Delia moved the family to San Juan, Puerto Rico shortly after his baptism. Adolfo's childhood was steeped in the teachings of the dark imaginings of his mother. She taught him the rituals of her bizarre religion even as he became an altar boy at the local Catholic church.

When Adolfo was ten, his mother moved her growing family back to Miami. They once again met with the Haitian priest and young Adolfo began an apprenticeship under the man.

A MOTHER FROM HELL

Adolfo's mother Delia was arrested over thirty times. Her rap sheet included shoplifting, passing false checks, grand theft and child neglect. Her punishment, however, was always lenient and she was never sentenced to anything more than probation. She attributed her ability to escape jail stints to the spells she cast under *palo mayombe* and she passed down this belief system to her son.

A true tenant from hell, she left every apartment she stayed in a vandalized mess. Delia left the walls and floors bloodstained with the remains of animals that she sacrificed. Living in a section of Miami known as the Coral Park Estates, Delia lorded over her neighbors in a reign of terror. Earning her reputation as a witch, Delia was vindictive with anyone who dared inspire her wraith. Neighbor Elena Menendez found a dead goose on her door step with its head wrapped in a red handkerchief. Carmen Reiganda opened her door to find a decapitated chicken on her porch after her son had gotten into an argument with Delia.

Mother and son left a legacy of fear behind in the small Miami neighborhood and the majority of the people were afraid to talk about them.

"Everyone here is worried (Adolfo)will come back to get them for talking," said one man. "I've completely protected my house, and if they come by, I'll blow them away."

LIKE MOTHER, LIKE SON

Adolfo inherited both his mother's religion and criminal ways. He indulged in Miami's gay bars during his teens and earned a living through petty theft. He found school to be a burden and was only interested in learning about black magic. The boy barely graduated from high school and dropped out of junior college after one half-hearted semester.

He continued to obsess about witchcraft with his Haitian priest mentor. They formed a team to rob graves at midnight to stock the priest's lair with dead bodies. They created voodoo dolls and sprinkled blood over them to curse people that crossed them.

The philosophical tenets of *palo mayombe* laid the foundation for Constanzo's future drug dealing endeavors. The belief system places no value judgments on the individual, there is no "good" or "evil" magic. Criminals familiar with the practice used it to protect them from the law but the Haitian priest had a solemn warning for his young student.

"Let the non-believers kill themselves with drugs," the priest said. "We will profit from their foolishness."

By the age of fourteen, Delia became convinced that her son had psychic abilities. Adolfo claimed to have predicted that President Ronald Reagan would be shot by John Hinckley. Adolfo had a murky vision for his own future, however, as he was arrested twice for shoplifting in 1981, including one incident where he tried to steal a chainsaw.

Two years later in 1983, Adolfo had sworn his allegiance to *Kadiempembe*, the name for Satan in *palo mayombe*. The Haitian priest gave Adolfo his blessing as the boy vowed to worship evil in return for financial gain. The priest initiated Adolfo into the fold with a ritual scarring as he took a knife and sliced arcane symbols into the body of his young student.

"My soul is dead," Adolfo said at the end of the ceremony. "I have no God."

BEGINNING OF A CULT

Blessed with good looks, Adolfo landed a modeling gig in 1983. He traveled to Mexico City for a photo shoot and earned some extra money telling fortunes with tarot cards in the city's dangerous Zona

Rosa (Spanish for "Red Zone", a strip of prostitutes, bars and drug dealings.)

The trip to Mexico netted him his first cult followers which included Martin Quintana Rodriguez, Jorge Montes, and Omar Orea Ochoa. Adolfo had affairs with Quintana and Orea, wherein he would be the "woman" or the "man" in the relationship depending on his mood.

In 1984, Adolfo moved his base of operations to Mexico City permanently. He lived with both Quintana and Orea, engaging in nightly homosexual ménage à trois. He began offering his psychic services around the city, developing a reputation for seeing into the future and offering *limpias.* These were ceremonial "cleansings" for those who thought they were cursed by life or wanted some enemies taken care of.

Adolfo kept records of his dealings with the townfolk and his journals revealed that he had thirty-one regular customers. Some of his patrons would pay up to $4500 for one single ritual. Adolfo gave his customers a menu in which they had a choice of sacrificial animals to choose from. Roosters went for $6, goats $30, boa constrictors $450, zebras $1100, and African lion cubs were $3100.

Adolfo began to target the more successful drug dealers in the area. He would help them schedule shipments and customers based on his own alleged "visions". He would charge exorbitant fees for his "magic" to make dealers and their henchmen invisible to police and remain bulletproof against would-be assassins.

Most of the drug merchants had upbringings that paralleled Adolfo's in that their parents were poor peasants who believed in the supernatural. They made for easy dupes for the charismatic cult leader who had one dealer pay him over $40,000 for his supernatural blessings over a period of three years.

Adolfo always delivered, however, as he realized that at such prices his magic would have to be just that, a magic show spectacle. On one occasion he and three of his followers broke into a Mexico City graveyard and excavated numerous graves for bones. His reputation grew as his stage show became more elaborate. He was soon entertaining physicians, business men, fashion models and a host of transvestite cabaret singers. In a bizarre twist, there were several high-ranking police officials that joined Adolfo's cult. The most notable was Salvador Garcia Alarcon, a lead narcotic investigator and Florentino Ventura Gutierrez who was the head of the Mexican branch of Interpol.

The devotion of these individuals clearly went beyond mere bribery or charm. It soon became apparent that they worshiped the young Satanist as he led them on a tour to all of the pits of hell he could dream up.

A year later, Ventura would introduce Adolfo to the infamous Calzada family, arguably Mexico's biggest drug cartel at the time. Letting his charisma do the work for him, Adolfo won the gang over with an elaborate ritual and they repaid him for his blessings of "magic". By 1987, Adolfo had amassed enough cash for a luxury condo and a slew of high-end cars which included an $80,000 Mercedes-Benz.

"Constanzo made these people believers," Gavito said. "I think it could happen to anybody. Most of these kids came from good families. And they're already involved in moving narcotics. So I think it was easy to graduate into the cult part of it. Because they saw the wealth and they saw the power that Constanzo had."

Adolfo liked to push the envelope, however. Not satisfied with his payments from the drug dealers, he disguised himself as a DEA agent and relieved a Guadalajara dealer of his cocaine stash. He sold the coke through his police connections for a $100,000 profit.

As the stakes rose, so did Adolfo's need to have more over-the-top rituals. It was during this time that he began incorporating human sacrifice into his ceremonies. His callousness in both torturing strangers and his closest friends scared both the dealers and police officials into remaining on his good side if they could.

The Calzada drug cartel bought into Adolfo's act hook, line and sinker. The simple minded drug dealers attributed their continued prosperity and survival to his magical powers. Adolfo sensed his influence over the family and realized that he had became a necessary "good luck" charm to them. In the spring of 1987, Adolfo called for a meeting with the heads of the Calzada family. He demanded to become a full partner in their drug dealing enterprise.

The Calzada family rejected the notion immediately.

Adolfo, however, realized that if he was not going to be given power then he would take it.

On April 30th, 1987 Guillermo Calzada Sanchez and six members of his family disappeared under suspicious circumstances. They were reported missing on May 1st with the authorities discovering remnants of what looked like a Santería ceremony at Calzada's office as they found as melted candles and bones scattered about. A week later, mutilated remains washed ashore on the Zumpango River. The police trolled the river and recovered the seven bodies. All of the corpses showed signs of severe torture: fingers, toes and ears were removed, genitals slashed, a spinal column was excised from one body, two others had their skulls opened with their brains missing.

The body parts of the Calzada drug cartel were now part of Adolfo's growing *nganga* or cauldron, a large iron kettle where he stirred up his "witch brew."

His primary drug competitors now eliminated, Adolfo believed that he was growing stronger in his dark magic and began setting his sights on bigger targets.

The Hernandez family became next on his to do list. Adolfo set up a meeting with the powerful Elio Hernandez through Sara who had been dating his son. Adolfo had received word that the Hernandez cartel had dissension in the ranks and were becoming more vulnerable to competing drug families.

During their talk, Adolfo convinced Elio of the efficacy of the *palo mayombe*. He seduced him with the idea of taking his enemies and sacrificing them to his Satan God. In return, Adolfo promised that his family and drug enterprise would be blessed by the dark forces, that they would become invisible to police and bulletproof.

"Give me fifty percent of the profits," Adolfo said. "And I'll control things."

THE BELIEVERS

In 1987, Adolfo became obsessed with a film called the *The Believers* which starred Martin Sheen and Jimmy Smits. It was a movie that showcased the Santeria and voodoo possession and Adoflo saw himself in the characters. He sought to replicate what he saw on the screen into his own rituals.

"It is not at all surprising that Constanzo and Sara Aldrete were infatuated with the movie *The Believers*," said occult researcher Carl Raschke. "The magical practitioners in the film are portrayed as insuperable and almost all knowing."

Adolfo saw the film as validation for what he was doing, specifically conjuring up the spirit realm to aid him in his crimes. Sara, on the other hand, used the movie as a recruiting tool for prospective members.

"[There is]...a story making the rounds that tells of the night Aldrete persuaded three male friends to screen a video of *The Believers*," Rolling Stone magazine reported. "After the film, say the students, Aldrete stood up and began to preach in strange tones about the occult. 'They had been drinking and they just thought she was trying to be spooky,' said one of the students who knew the boys. 'but they look back on it now and think she must have been serious.'"

THEY MUST DIE SCREAMING

Adolfo's thirst for more power and wealth required that his rituals become more specific and gruesome. He moved his cult to a place called Rancho Santa Elena which was about twenty miles away from Sara's hometown of Matamoros.

On May 28th, 1988, Adolfo murdered a drug dealer named Hector de la Fuente and a farmer named Moises Castillo in sacrifices to his demon God. Not satisfied with the level of sadism he achieved in those killings, he then tortured and mutilated a transvestite named Raul Paz Esquivel. Paz was a former lover of one of Adolfo's original followers, Jorge Montes. The level of torture was extreme as they dismembered Paz's body, turning him into a bloodied pretzel. Paz' dismembered body was then left on a city street only to be discovered by school children.

Sadism and torture became foremost on Adolfo's mind as he sought new ways to increase his depravity. Invariably, he would sodomize his victims before their death, giving them one last indignity. Blood and guts fed his cauldron where Adolfo turned the "stew" like a modern day witch. He believed that the devil he worshiped would be more pleased if his sacrificial victims suffered as much as possible.

"They must die screaming," Adolfo intoned to his followers.

THINKING BIG

On August 10th, 1988, rival drug dealers kidnapped Ovidio Hernandez and his two year old boy. They wanted revenge for being ripped off on an $800k deal.

Adolfo, feeling the need to show off the efficacy of his *palo mayembe*, kidnapped a random stranger off the street and brought him to the ranch. They tortured the man, offering him as a sacrifice to their Satanic God while praying for the safe release of the Hernandez family member and his son.

Three days later, the dealers released Hernandez and the boy without any ransom money being exchanged. The Hernandez family gave full credit to Adolfo and his use of witchcraft.

He had them under his spell...

NO SAMPLES FOR YOU

Three months later, a 35-year old ex-policeman turned cult member named Jorge Valente de Fierro Gomez was caught using drugs, stealing from Adolfo's stash.

Adolfo decided to make an example out of his follower as he didn't want any of his members to partake in the drugs. The ex-cop became yet another sacrificial offering to *Kadiempembe*.

On Valentine's Day of 1989, Adolfo's group captured three competing drug dealers and tortured them to death. They dismembered the bodies and added them to the gruesome brew. A week later, another sacrificial victim had been kidnapped but the man put up such a lengthy fight that the group was forced to kill him before he could be tortured. The followers continued their quest to acquire victims. They came upon a 14-year old boy and killed him before realizing that the teen was a cousin of Elio Hernandez.

The boy cried uncontrollably as Adolfo's henchmen had the knife to his throat. Adolfo decided that the boy could be added to the brew because he was too sad. If they sacrificed the boy, then the demon god would be sad. So they killed the boy and went out to the streets to find another young boy.

Adolfo did this because he wanted to acquire the boy's youth. When he wanted "youth" he would have a young boy kidnapped and sacrificed. When he wanted "strength", he would have a strong man kidnapped and dismembered into his brew.

SPECIAL BLESSING NEEDED

By this time, Adolfo had amassed over 800 kg of marijuana that his followers had stolen from another gang. He thought he needed a special blessing to ship the large amount across the Rio Grande. His followers kidnapped another stranger off the streets but Adolfo was not satisfied with the level of sadism they had achieved in torturing the man. He felt that his demon overlord, *Kadiempembe*, would require a new benchmark in torture and pain.

"Bring me someone I can use," Adolfo said. "Someone who will scream."

He also wanted someone smart, someone who had medical training. He instructed his followers to keep their ears out and find an American college student who was going into the medical field.

The next morning, his followers brought in a young college student named Mark Kilroy.

SPRING BREAK HORROR

Matamoros had been a popular hangout for college students on spring break for decades. Students would come upon the small Mexican city looking to let loose in the uninhibited foreign soil that offered prostitution, nudie bars, booze and drugs.

By March of 1989, however, the town had over sixty unsolved disappearances over the course of three months. Unfortunately, this did not deter the usual contingent of American collegians from descending upon the town and enjoying the nightlife.

Mark Kilroy was one of those tourists.

A popular high school student, he played on the basketball and golf teams. He served on the student council and graduated 14th in a class of 210. He initially enrolled at Tarleton State on a basketball scholarship but transferred to the University of Texas after two years, giving up his basketball aspirations to concentrate on his pre-med courses. He was, by all accounts, an upstanding young man.

His father, Jim Kilroy, recalled that when his son was in high school, he would sometimes go to Mark's bedroom to make sure he was studying. He would find the young man reading his Bible instead. "What do you do?" Kilroy asked as he recalled the memory of his son. "He needs to study. But do you go in and tell your son to quit reading the Bible?"

Mark had trekked to Mexico for the spring break with three friends who were all his former classmates at Santa Fe High in Texas.

"The whole semester," a friend recalled. "That (the trip) was all we talked about."

They spent the night enjoying the Mexican food and drinking. They chatted with some girls visiting there from Kansas then returned without incident to their rooms at the Sheraton Hotel on South Padre Island over 20 miles away.

The second night would be quite different. They spent the evening drinking and then around 2 o'clock in the morning they began walking toward the bridge which connected Matamoros with the Texas border town where they had parked their car. Two of Mark's friends walked ahead while Mark and Bill Huddleston lingered about twenty feet behind. Huddleston briefly stepped into an alley to urinate. Mark waited on the street.

When Huddleston came back onto the street he could not find Mark anywhere. There were no signs or sounds of struggle.

THE ABDUCTION

Four of Adolfo's followers had kidnapped Mark. They had been driving a red pick up truck along the main drag of Matamoros, tailing the group unnoticed.

When they spotted Mark alone, they offered him a ride.

"They all had badges that said 'state police,'" Gavito said referring to the fact that Adolfo's followers disguised themselves as cops. "They all had jackets that said police on them. They had red lights in their car. They ran around Matamoros like they were police officers. When (Mark) went off to use the bathroom that was the perfect time. They went up to him, they badged him, they put him in a car, they told him he was under arrest for being drunk. They drive down about two blocks. They pull over, they all get out, the policemen, the guys 'acting' as policemen. They wait for the other car to show up. (Mark) jumps out and starts running."

Mark Kilroy ran for two blocks. The Constanzo crew chased him down yelling "freeze".

"(Mark) being the well educated boy that he is," Gavito said. "Who was brought up to respect the law, when he heard the word 'freeze', he stopped. He was half a block from getting back on the main drag where there was two thousand kids partying. And he stopped, they handcuffed him, they threw him back in the car, they took him back to the ranch. They tied him up and they put him in the back of the Suburban."

He was given food and told he would not be harmed.

Twelve hours later, however, he would be sacrificed.

Kilroy was the only American kidnapped by the cultists. He also came from an affluent family including an uncle that worked for the U.S. Customs Service. His father was a chemical engineer and his mother a volunteer paramedic. The family were devout Catholics, active in their local church.

The response from from the public was immediate. There was a $15,000 reward for information leading to his return or the arrest of his kidnappers.

Yellow bows graced the churches of his hometown and beyond. Dozens of people joined the search for Kilroy, with hundreds of flyers being handed out around the town. San Antonio Mayor Henry Cisneros lobbied Mexican authorities to find the young man.

"I had worked with the Mexican police for over twenty years," Lt. George Gravito recalled. "Best cooperation you've ever had in your life. All of a sudden, I ran into a wall. No cooperation. The state police was telling us that (Mark) was involved in narcotics. But they wouldn't tell me where they're getting the information. This guy was corrupt. What we're meeting with right here on the border, one day you're investigating a crime in Brownsville, Texas and tomorrow morning you're investigating it in Matamoros, Mexico. It's not your jurisdiction and you have to know how to move around. You can't step on the wrong toes because they're gonna kick you out of the country."

The Matamoros police interrogated over one hundred known criminals in the area in the search for Kilroy. They beat their legs with clubs and sprayed soda water mixed with hot sauce into their nostrils.

They came up with nothing.

ONE MORE SACRIFICE

Adolfo had used the sacrifice of Kilroy in his mind to ensure the safe shipment of his marijuana. But now, he thought he needed yet another special sacrifice to his palo mayombe overlord.

Adolfo decided to target Sara's former boyfriend, Gilberto Sosa.

On March 28th, 1989, Sosa became the cult's final sacrifice as the marijuana made its way across the Rio Grande on April 8th.

Adolfo's alleged psychic abilities would fail him, however, as his depraved empire would soon come to an end in a way that he didn't foresee...

PURE LUCK

The police drew no leads for two weeks until they came across a "happy accident" on April 10th of that year...

"We were lucky," Gravito recalled. "What helped us in this investigation was, we had been working on some narcotic cases. DEA Brownsville had been working real close with *un commandante* in Matamoros. That *commandante* was Juan Benitez Ayala. He was the head of the federal police assigned to the Matamoros area. This man, Juan Benitez Ayala, I'll say was about five feet tall. But he probably stood about eight foot tall. I mean when this guy walked in anywhere people were scared of him. He worked and that's all he did.

"You didn't see him in bars. You didn't see him in restaurants. And the reason he didn't go to bars or restaurants, one, he was afraid someone might put something in his drink and kill him. The guy was taking down some powerful people in Mexico and we went to talk to him."

"I told him we got this problem with this state police guy, he says these kids were involved in narcotics, and I assure you that they weren't. We had helped them on some cases, we had busted some big people (because) we had shared some information. So he put his people to work. And every time we had a lead, we'd call him, we'd go over there, we'd kick doors down, you know, you don't need a search warrant, the search warrant IS the federal police and nobody gets in your way."

The Mexican police had erected roadblocks and began a random drug roust in areas of Matamoros unrelated to the Kilroy disappearance. They had a policy of targeting only the low level runners and leave the heads of the drug operations alone.

Serafin Hernandez was the epitome of the low-level drug dealer. He was the twenty year old nephew of Elio Hernandez and a well known trafficker. During this drug roust, Serafin came across the police checkpoint and was followed. He unknowingly led the officers to the innocuous looking cattle ranch. A shabby looking corral marked the front with a tar paper and wood shack that stood in the rear of the winding, unmarked road.

It was Rancho Santa Elena, the home of Constanzo's cult.

The police waited a week and returned en masse, arresting both Serafin and another dealer named David Serna Valdez. The interrogations began and the two dealers proved to be cocky witnesses. They claimed they were "protected" by supernatural powers, of course referring to the spells that Adolfo had cast.

Inside, the police found a horror chamber beyond the imagination of any snuff film. The 15x25 foot shed was saturated with blood and smelled of rotting flesh. They found human brains, hair, teeth and skulls. Some spines had been crafted into necklaces. Scattered around were machetes and white votive candles in a box that bore a picture of *Our Lady of Guadalupe.*

The press nicknamed Rancho Santa Elena as the "Devil's Ranch."

"I thought in my twenty two years of law enforcement I had seen everything," a Texas deputy said. "I hadn't. As we drew near, you could smell the stench...blood and decomposing organs. In a big, cast iron pot there were pieces of human bodies and a goat's head with horns."

MAKING THE CONNECTION

"About two o'clock in the morning I get a call from *el commandante*," Gavito recalled. "We found (Mark) he said. 'You found (Mark)? You kidding?' he said no. We found (Mark). Where? He said he's buried in a ranch outside of Matamoros. I asked him how? Or who? He said there was a caretaker that also lived near the ranch. When he arrested Serafin, he picked him up too, the caretaker, but he didn't file charges against him. But he kept him under house arrest and the caretaker saw a picture of (Mark) on top of the table. And he pointed to it and said 'I know that boy'. 'How do you know him?' 'I was feeding him. I was giving him bread. I untied one of his arms so he could sit up and eat' because they had him tied to the back of a Suburban."

El Commandante then began interrogating Serafin. Without prompting, Serafin began offering information on how he knew Mark Kilroy, admitting that he was the one who kidnapped him.

"This guy was volunteering all of this information," Gavito said. "I mean usually in Mexico you have to go, you know, I guess its something you have to know when you get arrested, that they're going to torture you to get the truth out of you. But I've never heard of anybody just confessing this easily as Serafin. And we kinda talked a little bit and the name Constanzo had come up on his investigations. Serafin had said that they had kidnapped (Mark) because the *Padrino*, Constanzo, wanted somebody who was studying medicine because they were doing some kind of witchcraft."

"They were going to use Mark's brain to give it to this pot that they had. And I didn't understand what he was talking about and I said did you have to torture this guy and he said 'no, this guy (Serafin) thinks that bullets do him no harm and the police can't hurt him he thinks that this guy, this Constanzo is gonna come in here and take him out of here."

"It's our religion," Serafin said. "Our voodoo."

George Gavito recalled that during Serafin's confession he repeatedly made reference to the aforementioned film, *The Believers.*

"I remember I didn't understand what he was telling me," Gravito said. "I said, 'Is it Santeria?' And he said, 'Yeah, yeah, Santeria, voodoo, man.' And then he kept on saying, 'The Believers, The Believers, The Believers.'"

"Elio made [Serafin] Garcia a priest, but Garcia didn't really know what he was practicing because all he had on his mind was the movie."

Serafin told the authorities about El Padrino, the Godfather, as being Adolfo Constanzo. He revealed the details of Adolfo's ritual of African magic, palo mayombe. "Adolfo ordered the slayings," Serafin said. He revealed that the Godfather had tortured and sodomized his victims before killing them. They would then mutilate the bodies and harvest the organs for his witches brew.

SCENE OF THE CRIME

Serafin was brought back to the Devil's Ranch with Ayala and Gavito, both police officials not expecting the level of depravity they were about to investigate.

"We asked him where the body was," Gavito recalled. "And he said 'which body?' Just like that. 'Which body?' 'Man,' El Commandante says. 'Man, if you're playing games with me' and he got pissed off. And he (Serafin) says 'hold on, which body you want?'"

"'What do you mean, which body!'" El Commandante screamed.

"There's a bunch of bodies out here," Serafin said. "Which one do you want?"

"What do you mean?"

"Yeah," Serafin began walking through the corrals. "There's one buried here, there's one buried there."

"How many?"

"I don't know."

"Where's Mark?"

"Over there in the corner."

"Where?"

"I don't remember exactly," Serafin said as he started walking to a corner of the corral. "But I think it is where that wire is."

The police looked down and saw a coat hanger half-buried in the dirt.

"Why a coat hanger?"

"Oh, because Constanzo wanted to make a necklace," Serafin said. "With Mark's backbone. So after we killed them and everything we ran wire through his back, through the spinal cord, so that later on we could just come and get it out and he could make a necklace."

Disgusted and angry, Benitez-Ayala handed Serafin a shovel, forcing him to dig up the body of Mark.

During the dig, Serafain revealed that Constanzo had killed Mark with one machete slice to the back of his head. He began revealing more details of other killings, matter of factly and without feeling. At one point he even asked if the police we're going to order food because he was getting hungry.

El Commandante Benitez-Ayala became enraged. He took out his Uzi and fired the weapon into the air out of frustration.

"You don't think bullets can hurt you?" he asked Serafin.

"No," Serafin replied.

El Commandante then began emptying his entire clip.

"That's when the kid's eyes opened up," Gavito recalled, remembering how frightened Serafin became. "I mean his eyes opened up when he heard that sound, I mean it freaked us all out because we didn't realize what was going on. He (Serafin) went from being a believer to being a disbeliever pretty quick. He went back to being a normal person."

Serafin suddenly snapped out of his brainwashed state.

"I don't know why they got us to do this," Serafin said.

"All of a sudden it was 'why' they got us to do this," Gavito said. "It just changed."

His body unearthed, Kilroy's skull had been split open and his brain removed. The police then found a nearby shed wherein they located Adolfo's *nganga*, a cast-iron cauldron that was stained with blood, body parts and numerous sticks, the "palos" of *palo mayombe*.

Inside the kettle were spiders, scorpions and the brain of Kilroy. His brain had been boiled in blood over an open fire along with a turtle shell, a horseshoe, a spinal column and other human bones.

FAILING MAGICAL POWERS

Adolfo was surprised at the reaction to Kilroy's disappearance. He was used to his killings not gaining any notoriety at all. Even after the fact, three of the unearthed victims have never been identified and only a handful were reported missing.

The next day, all hell break loose for the cult members. Four members of the Hernandez family were arrested and the cash from their big marijuana sale was confiscated. The police began unearthing bodies from the ranch on April 11th, finding more bodies in a nearby orchard.

Feeling the heat, Adolfo went on the run with Sara, and his two lovers Martin and Omar. A Hernandez family hit man named Alvaro De Leon Valdez, nicknamed "El Duby", came along as well.

Adolfo's first instinct was to go to Miami where he could be with his mother. He decided to stay travel to Mexico City, however, using the homes of followers and friends of followers to hide.

The gruesome discoveries made the rounds in tabloid television. Geraldo Rivera produced a segment on the murders. There were false sightings of the cult being reported in the United States. Adolfo was claimed to have been seen in Chicago where people mistakenly labeled him as part of the Windy City Mafia. Sara was reportedly seen skulking around schools throughout various border towns, threatening to kidnap and kill ten white kids for every one of her followers that were jailed in Mexico. There was a church located in Pharr, Texas that was burned down after rumors that some if its members were connected to Adolfo's cult. Serafin Sr, a drug dealer and follower of Adolfo, was found and arrested.

The national news did little to shed light on the whereabouts of Adolfo, however. They successfully hid from sight as if their Devil God had swallowed them up and welcomed them into hell...

BETRAYAL IN THE CARDS

Adolfo did a tarot card reading on April 18th, 1989 and supposedly foresaw a betrayal among his followers. He knew that any of the many low level drug runners could have ratted out Serafin Sr and he now looked at his followers with a suspicious eye. He kept a gun close by and did his best to avoid sleep. His paranoia led to angry outbursts against his acolytes.

"They cannot kill you," he warned. "But I can."

The Commandante, Juan Ayala, meanwhile, took the threat of Constanzo's *brujeria* (witchcraft) very seriously.

"He flew in his own brujo (male witch), to take care of him and to take care of all his agents," Gavito said. "To make sure there was not 'bad vibes'. And not only that, but to help him in the investigation. To find out what was the best way to catch Constanzo. He (the witch) told Benitez, 'you wanna catch him? Burn their hut! Burn their nganga! Burn where they were worshiping.'"

"So we got out there one Sunday morning. Took one Mexican television station to cover it because he wanted Constanzo to see this. The brujo puts gasoline around it. They light it up and it starts to burn and we sit there while the whole thing burns to the ground."

Adolfo watched the scene on television as Ayala had hoped. His screen police sifted through what was left at the ranch. He then went into a rage inside the small hideaway apartment, smashing furniture and flipping over the couch for starters.

"He felt raped," Gavito said. "He felt that we had invaded his privacy. That we had done something we shouldn't have. He started losing it."

MOVING ON

Adolfo made one last move with his followers as they found an apartment on Rio Sena in Mexico City.

Sara, finally realizing her life was in danger or needing to now play the role of the victim since the authorities were no doubt closing in, made a handwritten note. She threw it out the bedroom window in the hopes that a Good Samaritan would come along and find it.

The note read:

Please call the judicial police and tell them that in this building are those that they are seeking. Tell them that a woman is being held hostage. I beg for this, because what I want most is to talk—or they're going to kill the girl.

A stranger walking by picked up the note but kept it to himself, thinking it was a joke. Upstairs, however, Adolfo plotted his next getaway move.

"They'll never take me," he said.

MORE RANDOM LUCK

A few days later, police arrived on Rio Sena and began going door to door looking for a missing child. Adolfo saw them from his window and began opening fire with his Uzi not realizing that they were not looking for him.

Over one hundred eighty-police men almost immediately. A fiery battle ensued which lasted almost forty-five minutes. Surprisingly, the only person injured during the crossfire was an officer who was struck by Adolfo's first barrage.

According to Sara, Adolfo ordered his own killing, telling El Duby to shoot him and his right hand man, Martin Quintana Rodriguez.

"He lost it," Gavito said. "He turned on the stove. Put the money on the stove. Started burning money. He started throwing coins out. Just lost it."

"He went crazy, crazy," said El Duby. "He grabbed a bundle of money and threw it and began shooting out the window. He said everything, everything was lost. No one's going to have this money."

"He wanted to die with Martin," Sara said.

Adolfo soon realized he was trapped. He handed his Uzi to El Duby.

"He told me to kill him and Martin," El Duby said. "I told I told him I couldn't do it, but he hit me in the face and threatened that everything would go bad for me in hell. Then he hugged Martin, and I just stood in front of them and shot them with a machine gun."

The police entered the apartment with guns raised but Adolfo and Martin were already dead, their bodies slumped together in a closet. The three remaining cult members, El Duby, Orea, and Sara were captured.

Over twenty rounds were found in autopsied body, possibly indicating that the Mexican police had continued to shoot him port-mortem.

THE TRIALS

El Duby's case was open and shut. He had confessed to the two murders and had no reasonable defense. Sara, however, was a tad different as she initially proclaimed to be a victim but knew too much of the cult's ins and outs to not be considered an accomplice.

After the shootout, fourteen cult members in total were indicted for murder. In August of 1990, El Duby was convicted of the killing of Adolfo and Martin, getting a 35-year prison term. Juan Fragosa and Jorge Montes were convicted to 35 years for the killing of Raul Esquivel.

Omar Orea, one of Adolfo's lovers, died of AIDS before going to trial.

Sara had been acquitted of Adolfo's slaying but was sentenced to a six year term for her criminal associations. She maintained her innocence throughout, stating that she never practiced the *palo malembe* but a "Christian Santeria."

Showing a calm demeanor during her interrogations, Sara expressed sorrow for the murders of Kilroy and the other victims.

American law officials saw Sara as having a split personality. They knew that in private, Sara would lose her "charming aspect" that she revealed when she knew the television cameras were on. She reverted into another self, talking with relish in describing the cult's rituals.

"I would say she has three personalities," a Mexico City attorney general said. "One personality comes out and faces the cameras and denies any involvement in the human slayings, another emerges when she talks to police and the third one comes out when she talks to herself."

American Customs agent Oran Neck spent several days in Mexico City assisting the local police. "Sara has kind of lost touch with reality," Neck said after he questioned her. "Her dual personality is coming up pretty strong right now. When you talk to her without the TV cameras there, she's pretty truthful."

"She gives a lot of data with great detail to investigators. It seems like when the cameras come on, she kind of reverts back to this nice, young, clean-cut kid from Texas Southmost College."

"When the cameras were there, she was real nice," Lt. George Gravito said. "When she was with us, she was the same ol' witch."

SARA'S SENTENCE

"If I had known it (the cult) was like this," Sara said. "I wouldn't have been in it."

Six years after her criminal association sentence was up, Sara was tried again and convicted of several of the murders at the cult's headquarters. She is now serving 30 years in prison.

During an interview with SFGate, Sara claimed that she was tortured by Mexican police after her capture. She said she was stripped, blindfolded, hung upside down, beaten, had her toenails pulled out and was burned inside her vagina in and out. She claims the burns were so severe that a doctor told her she'd never have children.

She also remembers the police shoving her hands into Adolfo's autopsied body at the morgue.

They yelled at her to pull out his heart.

"There is your devil," they mocked. "There is your prince. Kiss him. Kiss him."

The Mexican authorities have denied these claims.

"The witch deserves everything she got," Lt. George Gavito said.

Mark Kilroy's parents have said they have forgiven her but do not want her released. "You have to control a mass murderer," said Jim Kilroy. "What are you going to do? Let her loose and have her murder other people?"

Even after the convictions, some murders from the time period have remained unsolved. Between 1987 and 1989, there were 74 unsolved ritual murders in Mexico City. 14 of these involved children. Adolfo's cult is connected to 16 but there has been no evidence to connect them to the rest.

"We would like to say, yes, Constanzo did them all," prosecutor Guillermo Ibarra said. "And poof, all those cases are solved. And the fact is, we believe he was responsible for some of them, though we'll never prove it now. But he didn't commit all of those murders. Which means someone else did. Someone who is still out there."

SATAN'S DAUGHTER NATASHA CORNETT

Natasha Cornett was born January 26th, 1979 in Pikeville, Kentucky.

Pikeville is located in the foothills of the Appalachian mountains. It is a mining town with most of its inhabitants devoutly religious.

"It's very beautiful scenery to grow up in," Cornett said. "But it's a suffocating place to live."

Born poor, Natasha was the product of an affair between her mother Madonna Wallen and her biological father, a police officer named Roger Burgess.

Her mother then left her husband, Ed Wallen, and raised Natasha alone. They lived in a trailer in Pikeville, Kentucky.

"She had energy to burn," her mother said. "She liked to draw. To read. She liked dogs and babies."

SCHOOL LIFE

Natasha was a good student in elementary school, behaving well and getting good grades. She seemed to be on the right path until one morning she found her mother laying unconscious. Madonna Wallen had overdosed on prescription drugs.

"My momma is on the bed naked," Cornett recalled. "With a bottle of pills laying next to her. I didn't know she was dying. It messed with me."

Around this time, Cornett's life began a downward spiral. She began suffering from anorexia. Then drugs. Then she began engaging in acts of self-mutilation, cutting her arms to "relieve her pain."

"Natasha started to engage in those acts as a means of getting control," forensic psychologist Roberta Nixon said. "She can control her diet. She can control her anger, or so she thinks, by cutting herself. She can control how she feels by doing drugs. Having a dim-witted mother certainly didn't help things either."

At one point, Natasha had lost over thirty pounds because of her anorexia as well as having over seventy cuts on her arms.

"I started cutting because I started going through a rough time with my mom," Natasha said. "It was a release."

"I don't know where that pain comes from," Natasha's mother, Madonna Wallen said. "She just says she has to do it to take away her pain."

In later court testimony, however, Wallen would admit to a history of physical abuse with her daughter.

"I used a belt one time and the buckles slipped from my hand," Wallen said. "And it hit her on the back of the leg. But it made a bruise on her."

Wallen later said that there was sexual abuse of Natasha by her husband whom she originally believed to be Natasha's father.

"Natasha had a really bad upbringing," C. Berkeley Bell, the District Attorney General for Tennessee said. "Lot of hard times. She came from a very dysfunctional family. Hard time in school. Was an outcast. Was ostracized by her classmates."

HIGH SCHOOL DROPOUT

Natasha entered high school but dropped out before her freshman year was complete. Her best friend was Karen Howell who would later be part of the "Wild Bunch" that Cornett would lead on a killing spree.

"Karen was my life raft," Natasha said. "She was the only person that understood me and let me be me. She knew my pain. She went through the same stuff."

Like Natasha, Karen had a dysfunctional family. Her father was an abusive alcoholic and her mother had a nervous breakdown. She came from a strict, religious family with her mother forcing her to stand on a Bible when she misbehaved. She was also bipolar.

"They were like two peas in a pod," Nixon said. "But in court interviews Natasha seems to more of a realization of what took place that night. Karen remained a petulant teenager, sullen and angry. Natasha was the better talker of the two so Karen followed her lead.

BIPOLAR DISORDER

Natasha was eventually diagnosed with bipolar disorder and in one episode had to be hospitalized at the Ridge Treatment Center in Lexington, KY. She had to leave the hospital after eleven days, however, as that was all the time the state health benefits would allow.

"Bipolar disease is brutal and even more so for people in low income circumstances," Nixon said. "It is extremely hard to treat. The amazing thing here is that she was only hospitalized for eleven days. After that, she doesn't appear to have gone through any kind of outpatient treatment program aside from an aborted session with a counselor. With people like Natasha, they need medication to keep their anxiety and impulses under control. Without it, anything can happen and anything will happen."

Natasha's mother began to see the rapid decline in her emotional state. Her choice of clothing would be reflect her mood and growing anger.

"From the seventh grade," Wallen said. "She just started changing. The big baggy pants. The rope with the emblems hanging. Everybody thought it was weird."

"I started drinking and smoking and associating with people that were weird," Natasha said. "You don't have to be perfect around them."

Natasha sought acceptance and eventually found it in the Goth subculture. Still, with the rapid mood shifts and change in dress, Natasha's own mother insists that there are three versions of Natasha.

"There is the sweet, caring girl," Wallen said. "There is the girl who would do anything for her friends, and there is a dark side that likes to play on a Oujia board, do seances and play vampire games."

MARRIAGE

At the age of seventeen, Natasha married Stephen Cornett. It was no ordinary ceremony, however. The bride and groom wore black and dog collars.

"We'd been friends for awhile," Natasha said. "It seemed like the logical thing to do."

The union only lasted a couple of months. Steven left without warning, abandoning Natasha. The dissolution of the marriage caused Natasha to spiral further into depression.

"It was awful," Natasha said. "I just kinda caved in on myself."

Natasha then fully immersed herself in the Goth subculture even further. She donned black clothing and listened intently to the dark, depressing music. She would pierce her eyebrows and lips with safety pins as well as use black lipstick and nail polish.

"For most kids," Nixon said. "The Goth culture is a way to rebel. To control their own image. It is a relatively harmless phase for most involved. They're young. They act out. Then they grow out of it. For some kids, however, like Natasha, it is more than that. She's disturbed to begin with and wants to take it beyond the dark music and black get-ups and really wants to do harm to someone. She realized that the Goth culture was a way to make people afraid of her. This is how she would gain power. She could control people by being their 'darkness consultant.'"

NATASHA THE VAMPIRE

She became a self-described "vampire" and named her black dog "Malkavian" after the vampires in her favorite vampire fantasy board game as well as collecting all of Anne Rice's vampire novels.

"She was a dark soul who'd give you the willies," a local teen said in describing her.

Natasha covered the walls of her bedroom in her trailer with numerous dark messages including "I hate the world" as well as drawing inverted crosses.

"Tasha would start hearing voices," Wallen said. "Talking to people on the Oujia board. Her and Karen fed on each other. You know. It just kept getting worse. She wanted away from all the people that called her 'freak.'"

Her drug use and drinking increased but she was able to attract a group of friends, most of whom looked up to her. The group consisted of three girls. The petite Karen Howell and the overweight, awkward Crystal Sturgill.

Sturgill was molested by her step-father and had been kicked out of her home. She needed a place to stay and hooked up with Karen and Natasha.

The threesome would go around the sleepy Kentucky town, spray painting pentagrams, the satanic number 666 and inverted crosses across the walls of buildings and homes.

"They were all sort of drop outs," reporter Bill Jones said. "Who fell through the cracks in school. They dressed in Gothic fashion, black clothing. Black make-up. Looks Satanic, if you're looking for Satanic that's what might come to mind."

"Everything that we did," Natasha said. "Was very destructive but also self-destructive. Nothing was done to harm anybody but ourselves."

Natasha began spelling her name backwards, 'Ah-Satan', spray painting it across the walls of the town.

"She used the name to intimidate," Dixon said. "In an odd way, that was part of her charm. She was more 'out there' than the impressionable kids in her town. She held sway over Karen Howell and Crystal Sturgill, both of whom were looking for someone they could look up to. So while Natasha was an outcast at school she was able to assemble other outcasts and cast them under her spell. She became the devil of choice to worship."

The gang carried around two books with them, *The Book of Black Magic* and the *Complete Book of Magic and Witchcraft*. The three girls would go to motel rooms or Natasha's mother's trailer to hang out, drink alcohol and each other's blood. They would also engage in seances and Satanic rituals they would read about in books.

"When it comes to the occult," Dixon said. "Most young people just dabble around with it. In the case of Natasha and her gang, however, she led them over the edge. They were dumb kids out looking for kicks and she pushed them into something that they probably would not have gotten involved in had it not been for her own dark compulsions."

ROAD TRIP TO HELL

"We're going to start armageddon," Natasha informed one of her friends. "I hate, therefore I am" became her mantra.

Natasha and the "Wild Bunch" decided to go on a road trip to New Orleans. They were obsessed with the vampire books of Anne Rice and thought about the prospect of meeting her. Talks began and the entire group wanted to leave the small town of Pikeville behind.

"All I could think of was I need out," Natasha said. "I need out. I need out. I need out. I can't breathe, I need out."

The group of girls were now joined by some equally nefarious young men. The first is Joe Risner who is Karen's boyfriend and at twenty years old, the oldest in the group. Risner, never knew his own father and was known as the quiet, introverted type. He wanted to impressed Karen but was insecure as his love interest seemed more infatuated with Natasha then with him.

Edward Dean Mullins was nineteen and the only one from the group that comes from an intact family that goes to church. He is struggling with self-esteem issues, however, as women reject him until he meets Natasha. James Bryant is fourteen but seemingly the most volatile of the "Wild Bunch". His mother has abandoned him and left him alone with an alcoholic father. Natasha and Karen met him on a street corner and picked him up because they thought he looked "cool."

Mostly likely, they saw him as someone the could use to do their dirty work.

"I had been friends with Joe for awhile," Natasha said. "Joe was dating Karen. Crystal needed a place to stay and she was friends with Dean (Mullins)."

Jason was the last entry into the "Wild Bunch." It was apparent, however, that he and Natasha didn't always see eye to eye. According to detectives, Jason was not as "controllable" as others in Natasha's group.

"Jason didn't make a huge impact on me," Natasha said. "He seemed dangerous. Like people pretend to be bad. I thought that was his hook. He was the 'bad boy.'"

Natasha's mother's trailer would be their primary hangout where they would drink, do drugs and later plot out their killing spree.

"Prior to leaving (for the road trip)," Bell said. "The defendants would watch 'Natural Born Killers.' That movie depicts individuals who are carefree, killing people. There don't appear to be from that movie, any consequences (to violence). They may have felt that there were not going to be any consequences for their actions. I really don't know what it takes for a group of people to take on that mentality of murder. They had no concept of tomorrow. Or consequences. And they just don't care."

The members of the gang become increasingly excited as they discuss the prospects of what will take place on their killing spree. Finally, they have some excitement in their boring, despondent lives with Natasha at the head.

"She seemed to be the leader of the group," Jones said. "And someone in the group said 'we're going to make headlines.'"

MOTEL SEVEN PIT STOP

The group piled into Risner's mother's car, a compact Chevy Citation. Before they would hit the highway, they rented out room number seven at the Colley Motel in Pikeville. Despite Natasha's apparent disdain for Jason, the young fourteen year old had cut

Natasha's initials into his arm that night at the motel. The group then attempted to burn the satanic numbers 666 into the motel carpet with candle wax.

They would then begin their self-mutilation ritual.

"Me and Karen started cutting," Natasha said. "And at first, it was just to cut. Then I wanted to die. I thought eventually if I cut myself so many times I would just bleed out. Mostly it was just me and Karen drinking each others blood. We just didn't do seances."

Crystal maintains that they were not part of a vampire cult or nor did they worship Satan. "We dressed in black and we'd stand out. And we did self-multilation. We were the freaks, the outcasts."

"We were trying to find answers, " Crystal said during in interview with Campus Life. "We all had been to church. It didn't provide answers. We were interested in Wicca, books on witches and spells. We were anarchists."

"They wanted to go to New Orleans," Natasha said. "Because that was the only place I was familiar with. And I said I wouldn't go back down there without some kind of protection."

Natasha was referring to the fact that she claimed to be raped in New Orleans although no charges were filed.

The motel owner, Jim Cochran, said that he rented out the room to Risner and described him as "polite and courteous". Risner, who also wore the Goth black make-up was described by detectives as "lanky and long-haired." A week before their killing spree, Natasha was in a Pikeville grocery store where she led Risner around by a dog chain fastened to a collar around his neck.

The group started a fire in the motel room and they were worried the manager would call the cops.

"Karen had just gotten into trouble," Natasha said. "And she didn't want to go back to juvenile. Jason just got out of juvenile and he didn't want to go back. And I was ready to run away at any given moment so it just kinda came together. We were all going to run away."

The group then vandalized and burglarized other Colley Motel rooms during their stay. They stole a television set and several pairs of work boots.

ROUTE 666

The group of disaffected youth drove to Forty-Acre Field, a remote campground where other teens would hang out. They started a campfire then at some point that night or early in the morning they burglarized two homes in a town called Paintsville. It was there they stole two semi-automatic handguns.

They thought about performing a carjacking as Joe's mother's Chevy Citation kept overheating. Nonetheless, they went onto U.S. Highway 23 south into Virginia.

The group was ticketed for speeding in Gate City, Virginia on April 6th but were allowed to continue on.

"Based on the evidence of what their stated purpose was," Bell said. "The night before they left. They were preparing to leave Pikeville. Go across the country. Robbing and killing people."

The group then drove into a used car lot and tried unsuccessfully to hot wire a vehicle.

They kept driving and an hour later, they stopped at the Interstate Highway 81 rest stop in Greeneville, Tennessee.

"Karen needed to pee," Natasha said.

Tragedy would ensue as the group came upon the Lillelid family at a truck stop in Greeneville,

THE LILLELID FAMILY

Thirty-four year old Norwegian Vidar Lillelid, his twenty-eight year old wife Delfina, their six year old daughter Tabitha and two year old son Peter were having lunch on a park bench.

Vidar, who worked as a hotel bellman, had taken his family to a religious convention in Johnson City. They were on their way home to Nashville. He had been in the USA for ten years. His wife, Delfina was a native of New Jersey but had parents who had immigrated from

Honduras. The two had married in 1989 and moved to Knoxville four years earlier from Miami because they wanted a nice place to raise their two children. The two were described as "devoutly faithful" and "humble" by those who knew them.

"The Jehovah's Witnesses were having a convention abut thirty miles north," Jones recalled. "They had been to that convention and they were going home. Jehovah Witnesses are known for being active in trying to recruit new members. They leave pamphlets and that sort of thing. That may have been the worst thing they could have done."

"I think they were doing a little proselytizing there," Bell said. "It was just part of their religion that they go out and try and talk to people. They saw the defendant's unusual appearance. They may have though that they needed some discussion about the Lord."

Vidar and Delfina approached the group and asked if they believed in God. Natasha spoke for the everyone, saying she dd not believe in God, as he had never come to her aid when she prayed as a child.

"The whole scenario just drips with tragic irony," Dixon said. "On one hand, we have the Lillelid family. They are sweet and naïve. They are following the dictates of their church to go out and invite as many members as they can for their church. Then there are these cult members who a diametrically opposed viewpoint. They have their own beliefs. Only theirs are something far more sinister."

KIDNAPPING AT GUNPOINT

According to Natasha, it was Joe who initiated the kidnapping of the family.

"It was when Joe said he wanted to converse with Vidar about his religious beliefs," Natasha said. "That just brought up red flags, because Joe was not a religious man. I tried to convince him (Joe) that we should just leave and get on our own way. Every step that he took, I was there trying to prevent it."

Natasha stated that it was never their intent to rob and kill the Lillelids. She became alarmed with Joe who went back to his car and got his gun. Then after conversing with Jason, Joe pulled the gun out on the Lillelids.

Detectives confirmed that Joe Risner admitted that he was the one that pulled the gun. Natasha remained steadfast in her own statement that she tried to stop Joe.

"He was like 'nothing is gonna happen,'" Natasha said. "'We just need your car.' All I could do was just look at them and apologize."

Vidar immediately offered his keys and wallet, pleading for the killers to not harm his family.

"They put them in their respective cars and took off," Bell said. "They got off the Interstate. Just a few miles down the road."

"I didn't think that the people that I was around could actually do anything bad," Natasha said. "Even Jason. I thought I could stop something."

Detectives found out otherwise, however. During interviews with the other members of the group, they believed that Natasha was the instigator. She was the one that members of the group thought could "draw on demons" and was the driving force behind the robbery.

Joseph Risner forced the family into the Citation. They drove along until they reach a remote area.

"It's a dead end, gravel, one lane road," Jones said. "They go down the end of that road and force the people out of the car."

The family is terrified. Vidar continued to plead for mercy. Young Peter is clinging to his mother's leg, his arms wrapped tight around her waist.

"This group of very strange looking people is surrounding them and laughing," Bell said. "And they see the weapon."

"I can't imagine what that would have been like," Jones said. "To know that your family was in peril like that."

According to Natasha, it was Risner that pulled the gun on the family but now on the deserted road it was Jason Bryant, the fourteen year old, who held the family at gunpoint.

"All of a sudden Jason pulled the gun up," Natasha said. "All I could see was rage on his face. And Joe walked away from it. He was like, 'I can't do that.' And I was like 'Jason, what are you doing? And he just started cussing. 'Get the fuck outta the way! Get the fuck outta the way! Move! Unless you wanna die, move!

"I got in between Jason and the family to where the gun was pointed at me and tried to convince him to not do that. I begged and I pleaded for what seemed like an eternity for him to stop. When I discovered that there was no stopping him, I begged for at least the children to be saved. He told me that if I didn't move, he would shoot me."

"I don't think I would have moved anyway until he promised and swore to me that he would not harm the children. That's when I moved. I didn't think that I could do anything to prevent it if I was dead."

During the testimony, Natasha, Risner and Karen Howell said that Bryant did the shooting. Bryant, however, said that Risner and Edward Dean Mullins fired the shots and later forced him to take the blame.

Gunpowder was found on Mullins, however. The detectives and prosecuting attorney believed that the entire group somehow were involved in the shootings as over seventeen shots were fired.

"If you wanted to be a member of this group," Bell said. "You had to participate in this ritualistic killing."

"I don't know which (of the family) got shot first," Bell said. "But the rest of them are observing their family being shot."

"The indication was that the children were shot last," Jones said. "The little girl had apparently walked around in her mother's blood. The boy even though he was two years old was shot in the head."

"I didn't watch," Natasha claimed. "I sat in the back of the van and just screamed. Please don't hurt them. Please don't hurt them. Please don't hurt them. Jason said 'Stop fucking crying.' He just laughed."

Six year old Tabitha was shot in the head. Peter was being held by his mother as he was shot. Each of the victim was shot in the eye as a 'signature' move.

"The males were shot in the right eye," Bell said. "And the women on the left."

"It was a ritualized killing," Dixon said. "Call it bonding through murder. They would hoop and holler and cheer each other on. "

The group left Risner's mother's car at the scene as it became stuck in the mud. They stole the family's van, the youths took off in the hopes of going to Mexico.

But not before they had dragged the bodies over, lying the four bodies parallel to each other so it appeared like a four-pointed star.

Joe laughed as they drove over the bodies, hearing the crunch of bone under the weight of the van.

THE AFTERMATH

Vidar and Delfina were found dead, tire tracks across their clothing. Tabitha was still alive when found but died en route to the hospital. Two year old Peter was shot in the torso and the eye. Amazingly, the boy survived although he is now blind in one eye and permanently disabled.

"Peter survived," Jones said. "The two year old boy had been shot through the eye with the bullet exiting the side of his head. It didn't kill him. He's disabled by the extent of his injuries. He had difficulty walking and of course, blind in one eye.

The youths showed no remorse after the shooting. People who lived nearby heard gunshots, laughing and shouting as they left the family for dead. The police were called and the Sheriffs discovered the dead bodies of the Lillelid family.

ON THE RUN

"After you witness something that atrocious," Natasha said. "I didn't know what to do."

The group went on the run, altering their plans to go to New Orleans. Instead, they headed to Arizona/Mexico border.

Two days after the shootings, Natasha and her cohorts were arrested by US Customs and Immigration officials in Arizona.

"They had been down into Mexico," Bell said. "And as they were coming back through the computers at the border had not been functioning. So the border could not check on who was coming in and out. But just as that group came back in the computer suddenly started working. And when they put the license tag in the system they got a hit. And they were arrested there in Arizona."

The detectives and defense attorney who dealt with Natasha after the arrest vary widely from her own well-thought versions of what took place that night.

"She was a vampire who worshiped Satan," said an officer who spoke to Natasha after her arrest. "She was on the dark side. Very bitter towards everyone."

Natasha allegedly told her first defense attorney, Eric Conn, that she was 'Satan's Daughter.' The attorney decided to play up that aspect of her defense as he hoped to get her a lenient sentence if she was declared insane.

"After Eric Conn got up in the devil worship and vampirism," Wallen said. "It kept getting worse and worse."

Natasha blames her first lawyer, Conn, for her lackluster defense.

"I don't know why it was me that was picked out of everyone else," Natasha said. "I know he did a lot of damage to me and my case.

"I didn't tell him that I even had any inclination toward that," Natasha recalled. "I knew he was a lawyer wanting to represent me pro bono. At no point had I ever been a satanist. Ever. Once something like that is said. You can't just take it back."

Conn was later replaced by Stacy Street but the damage had been done.

Natasha's current court-appointed attorney stated that "he (Conn) volunteered to represent her, then immediately began negotiating movie rights.

SOUVENIRS OF A KILL

"Each one of these killers," Berkeley said. "Took an individual trophy from their victims. And kept it attached to a chain or a wallet."

Karen Howell took Vidar's social security card and Tabitha's 'Hello Kitty' merchandise. Natasha took Tabitha's social security card and her wallet. Sturgill had taken the keys to the Lillelid home all for souvenirs.

DEATH PENALTY?

"We were very concerned that the proof might focus on the juveniles as being the shooters," Bell said. "Juveniles can't get the death penalty. And if they can't get the death penalty we were concerned that no one else would get the death penalty either. What we reached was an agreement that we'd have a hearing."

A media circus followed the trial as an angry mob descended upon the teenagers as they entered the courtroom.

"Someone yelled that I was Charles Manson's daughter," recalled Sturgill.

In the trial, all six defendants had different stories as to how events took place that night and who pulled the trigger.

"It is my position that it was part of an initiation," Bell said. "That everybody had to participate in the shooting."

"Natasha clearly was the ring leader in all of the killings here," Dixon said. "She was the most articulate and confident of the group. The young men in the group were all shy types, eager from some female validation, with the possible exception of Jason who was a budding psychopath. But again, he was a dim-witted fourteen year old pitted against a smooth-talker in Natasha. Sturgill and Howell looked up to Natasha in their own ways as well. Sturgill was social awkward, overweight. She finally found people she could call friends and would do whatever they said. And Karen would not become violent on her own. These individuals were all like that, they could be violent but needed someone to light the fuse. And Natasha struck the match for everyone.

CONVICTION

Natasha was convicted on March 13th, 1998 with the five other youths. She reached a plea bargain where she plead guilty to all of the charges to avoid the death penalty.

In her court testimony, Natasha maintained that she was not the shooter of the four victims. She kept asserting that she tried to prevent the deaths of the Lillelid family members.

All of the defendants were sentenced to three life terms plus twenty-five years without the possibility of parole.

"She wasn't the shooter," Natasha's mother said, maintaining her daughter's innocence. "She got the same thing as the shooter."

PRISON LIFE

Natasha is housed at a prison in Nashville. She has earned her GED and her mother Madonna claims that her daughter serves as a "mentor to fellow inmates as they work to earn their GED."

"I was a teacher's aide for about a year," Natasha said during a newspaper interview.

Her troubled times continued, however, as on August of 24th 2001, she and death row inmate Christa Pike allegedly attacked a fellow prisoner named Patricia Jones.

They tried to strangle Jones to death with a shoe string after all three were placed in a holding cell with Natasha during a fire alarm.

Pike was on death row for torturing and beating a woman to death when they were Job Corps students in 1995.

Another inmate, the twenty-year old Jennifer Szostecki started the fire which created confusion during the fire alarm. This allowed Christa Pike to gain access to Patricia Jones.

Jones allegedly teased Pike about her upcoming execution.

"All she does is snitch on me and stab me in the back," Pike said during a phone call with her mother.

Natasha allegedly struggled with Jones before Pike came from behind and started to choke Jones with the shoe strings from a hiking boot. Natasha was Pike's friend and Szostecki's "girlfriend."

Letters filed in criminal court show Szostecki's obsession with Natasha.

"I love you," Sozstecki wrote. "I hate you. I miss you. I want you. I need you."

Pike was later charged with attempted murder while there was insufficient evidence to charge Natasha.

"I expected big women with shanks and stuff like that," Natasha said of her time in prison. "You know, like that typical prison scene that you would see in a movie. But it's not like that. You just get up, go to meals, have an hour out for recreational purposes and watch television and read."

PETER LILLELID

Peter Lillelid would be the subject of a custody battle between his USA based relatives and his aunt in Sweden. His aunt and uncle from Sweden won custody and Peter was sent to be in their care.

They kept him shielded from the media and he does not like to read the accounts of what happened to his parents and sister.